WORKING THROUGH
MENOPAUSE

THE **IMPACT** ON **WOMEN,** **BUSINESSES** AND THE **BOTTOM LINE**

MACHE SEIBEL, MD AND SHARON SEIBEL, MD

FOREWORD BY JOANN V. PINKERTON, MD

Executive Director Emeritus
The North American Menopause Society

Dedication

This book is dedicated to Dr. Philip and Lorna Sarrel who have dedicated their careers to women's health and menopause in particular, and who have pioneered advocating for women who are working through menopause.

OTHER PUBLICATIONS BY ONE OR BOTH OF THESE AUTHORS

Infertility: A Comprehensive Text

Family Building Through Egg and Sperm Donation
with Susan Crockin

Technology and Infertility
with Judith Bernstein, Ann A. Kiessling, and Susan R. Levin

Ovulation Induction

Infertility Your Questions Answered
with SL Tan and Howard Jacobs

Journal Babies
Your Personal Conception and Pregnancy Organizer
with Jane Stephenson

Save Your Life
What To Do in a Medical Emergency
with Shelly Glazier

A Woman's Book of Yoga
Embracing Our Natural Life Cycles
with Hari Kaur Khalsa

The Soy Solution for Menopause

Eat to Defeat Menopause
with Karen Giblin

The Estrogen Window

The Estrogen Fix

The Hot Years Magazine
HotYearsMag.com

Published by
HealthRock® Publishing
Newton, MA

ISBN 978-1-66780-764-5
eBook ISBN 978-1-66780-765-2

The authors have made every effort to present accurate and up-to-date information in this book, but they cannot guarantee that the information is correct or will suit your particular situation.

Limit of Liability and disclaimer of Warranty: The publisher has used best efforts in preparing this book, and the information provided herein is provided "as is."

Medical Liability Disclaimer: This book is sold with the understandingthat the publisher and authors are not engaged in rendering any legal, medical or any other professional services. If expert assistance is required, the services of a competent professional should be sought.

This book is presented solely for educational and entertainment purposes and the authors and publisher make no representation or warranties of any kind and assume no liabilities of any kind with respect to the accuracy or completeness of the contents and specifically disclaim any implied warranties of merchantability or fitness of use for a particular purpose. Neither the authors nor the publisher shall be held liable or responsible to any person or entity with respect to any loss or incidental or consequential damages caused, or alleged to have been caused, directly or indirectly by the information or program constrained herein. No warranty may be created or extended by sales representatives or written sales material.

The legislation quoted in this book relates to the United Kingdom and the United States identified as of this writing and are not represented as an exhaustive listing. The principles of making reasonable adjustments and taking a strategic approach in managing employers at menopause in the workplace are applicable worldwide.

Every company is different, and the advice and strategies constrained herein may not be suitable for your situation. You should seek the services of a corporate professional before beginning any improvement program.

TABLE OF CONTENTS

FOREWORD

Have you noticed any of the following about yourself, someone you love, or one of your coworkers? Hot flashes or night sweats, mood swings or being more irritable, lowered libido or vaginal dryness, sleep disturbances, adult acne, weight gain, or the difficult feelings of brain fog, forgetfulness, or decreased concentration? No, these are not a sign of a medical illness nor a sign of impending dementia. However, you may want to seek support and medical advice about perimenopause and menopause.

"Put facts ahead of emotions." "You can't fix what you don't know." The author of this book, Mache Seibel, made these statements in a The Hot Years Magazine (HotYearsMag.com[1]) interview by me in 2019, following his recovery from a life-threatening illness. However, these same statements apply to his and his wife's approach about why businesses need to focus on supporting menopausal women in their workplaces. Going through the menopausal transition affects women, their health, and the bottom-line financial gain for companies. Groundbreaking research and real-world testimonials explain how every workplace needs to develop support for menopausal women. I hope this book will enable you to actively support and champion women transitioning into menopause in your workplace.

Providing support for women in menopause is about helping women transition through a time of fluctuating hormones to find the "postmenopausal zest" that Margaret Mead mentions. I am a nationally recognized menopause specialist involved in teaching and researching new menopausal therapies to provide women access to medical information and the resources they need to stay healthy and vibrant as they transition to the second half of their lives. I am a full professor in the Department of Obstetrics and Gynecology at the University of Virginia Health System. I taught my male chairperson about the need to keep Kleenexes in his office as tears often came without warning and from both praise and constructive criticism. There was no support available to help me when I went through menopause or to help me learn how to balance work and life.

The authors of this book are a married duo. Dr. Mache Seibel is an international expert on women's menopause and a Harvard Faculty member. He is the recipient of multiple awards, including the Media Award from the North American Menopause Society for advancing the knowledge of menopause, the recent 2020 Healthline's Best Menopause Blog, serves as editor of the award-winning Hot Years Magazine. In his books, *The Estrogen Window* and *The Estrogen Fix*, he expertly explains menopause. He describes the window of opportunity for estrogen therapy to lower the risk of breast cancer, heart disease, and Alzheimer's disease while minimizing common menopausal symptoms of hot flashes, night sweats, mood swings, lower libido, fractured sleep, brain fog, irritability, and weight gain. He is joined by his wife, Dr. Sharon Seibel, a Harvard-trained psychiatrist with over 35 years of experience in the medical field and co-editor of The Hot Years Magazine.

I first met Mache and Sharon Seibel when they interviewed me for their national video series. Mache always asked me questions that challenged me to explain why the new research findings were essential to his viewers. Later, when I served as executive director for the North American Menopause Society, I appreciated how Mache and his wife picked the most up-to-date research as topics and the experts to interview who could explain the research findings and the impact of the study. He clearly deserved the NAMS Media award for all his work getting out the word on new menopausal research.

One year I had the pleasure of reversing the role and becoming the interviewer when I interviewed Mache following his stem cell transplant in a video titled "How to Deal with Illness." He said, "If something is wrong, look into it." "Get a diagnosis, and then research your care and your provider." "Put the information ahead of your emotions." That is what they have done in this book. They identified a critical problem that working women need support as they transition through menopause. They researched the answers and then put facts ahead of emotions with documents and testimonials used to present practical suggestions for women and businesses to take away the glass ceiling of menopause currently present for women in the workplace.

The North American Menopause Society suggests that by 2025, more than 1 billion women worldwide will be postmenopausal.[2] In addition, almost one-fourth of the US workforce is in perimenopause or menopause—with less than ten percent adequately treated. Many women don't understand the connection between the symptoms they are experiencing and the transition into perimenopause. Their symptoms come from the fluctuating hormones leading up to menopause and may last 5-10 years, and ends with menopause, defined as no period for 12 months. There is a shroud of secrecy around women's intimate bodily functions, which leads to a lack of public knowledge and discussion about women's health in midlife, a taboo topic. Women don't discuss it because they fear being stigmatized and ridiculed for it.

The workplace is often unaware of the impact menopause is having on its workers. The workers are often silently dealing with the experience of perimenopause and the wide range of mood changes that may occur while potentially dealing with stresses of life at home—teenagers, aging parents, partner issues, and work stress. Menopausal symptoms can have a profound effect on how a woman feels physically and emotionally. Self-confidence may be eroded, and some question if indeed they are going crazy or losing their minds. All of this can affect workability. Moreover, many women suffer in silence, feeling isolated, not talking about their symptoms, and not seeking help until there is a work, family, or relationship crisis. At work, women fear that their symptoms will not be taken seriously or that admitting to them will threaten their job security or chances of promotion.

When seeking help, many women find harmful misinformation, partial truths, persistent myths, and old wives' tales that affect their ability to take appropriate action. Not addressing the menopause experience carries health risks of accelerated aging, bone loss and fracture risk, higher cardiovascular risk, and worsening anxiety or depression. What results is often incorrect treatment, fear of treatment, no treatment, or inaction. We need to help find compassionate, knowledgeable quality care for menopausal women and discuss the emotional impact of menopause on them, their families, and their work.

I asked Mache and Sharon what they hoped readers would take away from this book. They said that the lack of support for women transitioning through menopause is a "glaring deficiency in the workplace." They believe that being proactive in providing support for women during this challenging transition time might prevent future litigation and help the company with employee retention, satisfaction, and productivity. Moreover, addressing it would help both women and businesses. In turn, this will help the company's bottom line. Not caring for menopause symptoms and preventing menopause-related disease leads to medical treatment costs, workplace lost productivity and may affect performance just when women are moving into leadership roles, thus leading to the glass ceiling of menopause.

Mache and Sharon are correct that the time is right to affirm menopause as a health condition that affects women and businesses. I sincerely appreciate their contributions to women's health and hope that this book will trigger needed changes in the workplace for women and their companies. Let us work together to transform menopause into a time of growth, learning, and excitement as women mature to become even better workers and seasoned leaders.

JoAnn V. Pinkerton, MD.

JoAnn V. Pinkerton, MD

Professor of Obstetrics and Gynecology

University of Virginia Health System

Charlottesville, Virginia

Executive Director Emeritus, The North American Menopause Society

INTRODUCTION

Shining a Spotlight on Menopause at Work

Ginger Rogers did everything Fred Astaire did,
only in high heels and backwards.

– Robert Lee Thaves

Menopause isn't typically talked about at work—it should be. Half of women in the workplace, one fourth of all workers, are experiencing menopause. Maybe even you.

This book is for you if…

- You are a woman
- You are transgender
- You work with women
- You are an employer who employs women
- You are a legislator or policy maker who represents women

This book was written to shine a light on a glaring deficiency in the workplace that is impacting women, businesses, and the bottom line. It is doing so while hiding in plain sight—a taboo topic that almost no one is talking about it. Working Through Menopause will help you discover what can and should be done to make the workplace a better, more productive menopause experience.

Each day, an estimated six thousand women in the United States enter menopause. That's 1.3 million women each year coming to a cubicle near you. Although the mean age of menopause in the United States is fifty-one years, the range of entering menopause is forty-five to fifty-five years of age. An additional five to ten percent of women will enter menopause before the age of forty-five years (early menopause) and one percent will enter menopause before age forty years (premature menopause).[3] The symptoms can start up to ten years before that. Then there are the millions of previvors, women who possess a gene mutation that increases their risk of cancer, and proactively have their ovaries removed (surgical menopause) in their thirties or early forties to lower their cancer risk. Millions more women have their ovaries damaged from radiation or chemotherapy from cancer treatment.

Just behind all those women are the millennials, the oldest of whom are now forty years of age, right on the cusp of the perimenopause/menopause experience. When you stop to think about it, menopause is not about age, it's about transition. Most forty-year-olds aren't connecting the dots between the symptoms they are experiencing and their transition into perimenopause—the hormonal imbalance that precedes menopause and lasts up to ten years. More and more women at work are either entering or in menopause and experiencing symptoms, many without awareness of what's causing it, or that menopause is even happening. Of all those millions of women, approximately seventy-five to eighty percent will have symptoms, and less than ten percent are adequately being treated. That means that the vast majority are coping with their symptoms at work without any intervention, without talking about it, and without the workplace offering either support or solutions. This represents a very large segment of the workforce whose work experience and performance are being greatly impacted. Menopause is a silent ceiling.

We have used many scientific references to define, explain, and support our opinions, but this topic is at the interface of medicine, health and wellness, business, law, and society, and actively evolving. For that reason, we have incorporated a number of references from a variety of news, legal, and business sources as well as medical resources.

Working Through Menopause was written to reframe menopause as a normal part of life, an extension of the reproductive portion of a woman's life, a normal part of the workplace, and something that every woman will experience if she lives long enough. It is not shameful. It is not something that has to be endured and not addressed. It should not be the taboo topic in the workplace, or anywhere else, that it has become. Quite the opposite. With women representing roughly half the workforce, and approximately forty-five percent of those women in perimenopause or menopause, we are talking about many women at the prime of their careers who are having a menopause experience while at work. These women are critical to the workforce and need support.

This book will explain why putting proactive menopause policies and programs in the workplace to support the menopause experience will improve work ability, retention, employee happiness, and business's bottom line. It will also lower a company's legal risk. Our goal is to get the conversation started to create beneficial change for both women and business.

CHAPTER 1

The Many Faces of Menopause – Three Case Studies

At puberty a woman meets her power,
During her menstruating years she practices her power,
At menopause she becomes her power

– Native American Saying ~

If you were asked to describe what the typical woman in or near menopause looks like, what would you say?

Before you give it too much thought, be forewarned. Whatever you say will largely be inaccurate. The "typical" woman in menopause is as varied as the fifty million women in menopause in the United States and the 1.2 billion women in menopause worldwide. They are young and old, thin and heavy, short and tall, trying to have babies, trying not to have babies, or can't have babies, minimally affected by symptoms and hugely affected by symptoms.

However, if you were asked to describe the stereotype of a woman in menopause, one survey suggests an unflattering answer that would include terms such as "not very sexy," "not very pretty," "not very tech savvy..." just..."not very..."[4]

This is not a very positive generalization, and one that couldn't be more inaccurate, as evidenced by just a few of the well-known women in menopause listed below who are openly willing to admit it…and to talk about it:

- Michelle Obama
- Oprah Winfrey
- Angelina Jolie
- Gwyneth Paltrow
- Belinda Carlisle

To give you a window into the many faces of menopause in the workplace, meet Jennifer, Rachel, and Marie—representing three composite examples of menopausal experiences. Perhaps you'll recognize some of your experiences in these descriptions. These women went through their transitions at different ages and each struggled with a different experience that affected both their lives and their work. The good news—all of these women could have been helped with appropriate education, support and intervention.

Jennifer's Story.

Jennifer was thirty-five years old and a rising star in a management consulting firm. Her grades and personality landed her a job right after graduating with an MBA from business school. She was quickly identified as a talented manager with the interpersonal skills and business smarts to eventually become a partner.

Jennifer had married five years earlier and was always looking for the "right time" to start her family. At thirty-three her job was secure, so she decided the "right time" was "right now." But when month after month went by without success, she grew increasingly anxious.

After a year without conceiving, Jennifer shared with her Ob/Gyn, "I really want to have a baby. But my periods are becoming slightly irregular, and work keeps getting busier." After more discussion and an exam, the doctor responded, "It's probably because you haven't gotten pregnant and your workload has gotten harder to manage. I mostly deliver babies, but I'm willing to prescribe you clomiphene citrate. It's a common, oral fertility medication. Let's try that for a few months and see where we are." After taking the medication for six months, Jennifer still wasn't pregnant.

Jennifer's husband noticed she had become even more anxious and a little depressed. She was also having difficulty sleeping, which caused her to feel increasingly tired. He thought it was because she was working so hard. It wasn't just her husband who noticed that something seemed different. At work, Jennifer was less engaged with her clients. Her supervisor observed that she was billing fewer hours per week and didn't speak up as often at meetings like she had in the past. Jennifer also forgot to call a client back, which was very unusual for her. The supervisor asked Jennifer if she was having any problems. Her work was still of high quality, but there was a noticeable difference in her level of involvement at staff meetings and in her performance. Jennifer confessed she was trying to have a baby, and since the supervisor wasn't sure how to respond to that, he awkwardly backed off.

Jennifer's Ob/Gyn referred her to a fertility specialist and after a consultation and appropriate testing, Jennifer was told a few weeks later at a follow up visit that she was going into premature menopause, a term used when menopause occurs before age forty. You could hear the air rush out of Jennifer and see the blood drop out of her face. "How could that be? I exercise regularly, eat healthy... and most of all, I haven't even had my first baby." It was a box of Kleenex conversation.

Jennifer was placed on birth control pills, not to prevent her from becoming pregnant, but as a short-term form of estrogen therapy. After further discussion, she and her husband decided to try to conceive by egg donation, which involves in vitro fertilization using an egg from a fertile egg donor fertilized with her husband's sperm. The first cycle was unsuccessful, but after the second cycle, at the end of her thirty-sixth year, Jennifer was in menopause, and the new mother a healthy baby girl.

After the delivery, Jennifer was placed on hormone therapy. When she returned to work following a three-month maternity leave, her supervisor and colleagues were delighted to realize Jennifer was performing at her previous level of engagement and high-quality work (minus being tired as a new mom). The next year, Jennifer was promoted to full partner.

Rachel's Story.

Rachel was forty-five years old and a personal trainer. Given her profession, she thought she knew her body pretty well. She was in great shape, loved her work, and had run in several marathons. But at age thirty-nine things began changing. She was tired all the time and especially exhausted after working out. Things had changed to the point she would sometimes call in sick just to avoid going to work. Worst of all from Rachel's point of view, she had started gaining weight. Suddenly, she had a tummy and was losing her waist line. Her periods were getting heavier and at night sometimes she would wake up hot and sweaty, feeling like a hot mess.

Rachel had visited her doctor several times looking for answers but the testing was inconclusive, and the doctor kept telling her over the past few years that nothing could be found, so she stopped going back. Rachel became increasingly anxious and depressed. One day while working with one of her fitness clients, the woman asked Rachel if she planned to run in this year's marathon. Rachel stiffened and something just snapped. Rachel spewed out a few very inappropriate comments, which were not typical of her usually friendly disposition. The client was not amused, stormed out, and reported Rachel to the front desk.

"I feel like such a bitch," Rachel apologized to her supervisor. "That's just not me." She called the client and apologized to her as well. To make things worse, Rachel forgot to write down her client's progress at the end of the workout. Rachel wished she had taken a leave of absence when she started thinking about it a few months ago, but the fitness center was understaffed and they begged her to stay. Turns out she may now be fired.

Rachel went back to see her doctor who placed her on an antidepressant. Shortly after that she told one of her girlfriends about what had happened. "I just feel totally out of control," Rachel confided. "It's not like me. Maybe I'm losing my mind."

"You're not losing your mind," her friend responded.

"I was feeling like, 'Who has inhabited my body?' Turns out I'm in perimenopause. My doctor explained I'm getting close to menopause and my hormones are out of balance. So I'm feeling and acting kind of whacky."

Armed with that information, Rachel went back to talk with her doctor. She had gained fifteen pounds in the past two years, which was really upsetting to her as a fitness trainer. When the doctor asked when she had her last menstrual period, Rachel realized she hadn't had a period in just about a year. The doctor rechecked her blood tests. This time they were conclusive. Rachel wasn't losing her mind. She had just entered menopause.

Marie's Story.

Marie was fifty-five years old and the president of a large urban hospital. She had started her career in another hospital as a nurse and worked her way up the chain of command, from a staff nurse to nursing supervisor, to Vice President of Quality. At each level, Marie excelled and continued to be promoted. Five years earlier she had been recruited to her current hospital to take on the role of Chief Operating Officer. When the current president and CEO was ready to retire, he highly supported Marie to take the reins of the hospital from him.

It hadn't been an easy rise to the top, though Marie made it look easy. As a woman she had a different style of managing and saw things differently than many of her male coworkers. She was known for her even handedness and willingness to compromise to get the key objectives accomplished. While she worked hard to collaborate, she walked a fine line to never look weak or emotional. There weren't a lot of other women at her level to confide in. The *hospital was always profitable and was always ranked as one the top hospitals in the state. Marie was a rock star.*

However, over the past few years she didn't feel like a rock star. She started having palpitations and went to see a cardiologist who told her that her heart was normal. Her bladder was getting progressively more sensitive, which made it hard for her to complete a meeting without excusing herself for a bathroom break. She made a note to schedule an appointment with a urologist. Marie knew many of the workers in the hospital by name and she liked to address them by name to create a warmer relationship. Sometimes she could not think of a person's name, even though she had known them for years. "Maybe I should see a neurologist," she told her husband one evening. "I hope I'm not getting dementia."

The thing that upset Marie the most was fairly new but happening increasingly often over the past few months. When she was leading a meeting and someone put her on the spot, or said something that was getting under her skin, her upper chest, neck, and face would become red and blotchy. It was a "tell" so that others knew when they had scored a point. She would also come home at the end of the day totally exhausted, a feeling she wasn't used to.

Marie had been seeing her primary care doctor each year, but it seemed none of these things had been asked about. She found herself feeling more and more frustrated and upset. The same workload was becoming increasingly more challenging. It caused her to question her ability and to get less satisfaction from her work. She considered whether or not it was time for her to step down.

By now you may have guessed, Marie had entered menopause.

Bottom Line: These three composite faces of menopause illustrate that menopause affects women differently. A subset of women will sail through menopause without symptoms and feel relatively unaffected, but that is not the typical situation. The symptoms are varied and, in some cases, quite significant. That's why it's so important for employers to have an understanding of this topic and have flexible policies, procedures and training in place to address these issues. And access to resources to support the menopause experience.

CHAPTER 2

The Silent Ceiling

There is no greater agony than bearing an untold story inside of you.

– Maya Angelou

Menopause is happening and no one is noticing

When it comes to menopause at work, neither women nor businesses are giving it the attention it deserves. That's why we're calling working through menopause a "silent ceiling." Like the glass ceiling, first introduced by Marilyn Loden in 1978, menopause impacts both the quality of women's lives and their ascent in the workplace.[5] All of this is occurring with little fanfare, recognition, or discussion.

That has to change and the sooner the better. Women and businesses need information and support during this normal but impactful transition. It's not only the right thing to do for women, it will also greatly benefit the bottom line of the businesses where they work.

The Harvard Business Review summarized the impact of menopause on women in the workplace very nicely:

Menopause often intersects with a critical career stage. It usually occurs between ages forty-five and fifty-five—which is also the age bracket during which women are most likely to move into top leadership positions. Since menopause generally lasts between seven and 14 years, millions of postmenopausal women are coming into management and top leadership roles while experiencing mild to severe symptoms such as depression, anxiety, sleep deprivation and cognitive impairment, to name a few. If we want to continue to move the needle on the number of women in leadership roles and maintain their valuable contributions to a company's bottom line, we need to be more open about what menopause is and how it affects both individuals and organizations.[6]

Menopause in the Workplace is Common

You may be thinking, "Hmm, interesting, but menopause is such a small niche." If so, you're thinking would be inaccurate. Roughly half the workforce in Canada, Australia, Sweden, the Netherlands and the UK is made up of women.[7] Women make up at least forty percent (mean 45.4 percent) of the workforce in eighty countries.[8] In the United States, the US Department of Labor reports that women are just over half the workforce.[9] Of those women, 20.1 percent are aged forty-five to fifty-four (15.5 million women), 17.3 percent are fifty-five to sixty-four (17 million women), and 8.1 percent are aged sixty-five and up (6.2 million). All together that is 45.5 percent of US women at work either in or approaching menopause. Another 21.1 percent of the female workforce is aged thirty-five to forty-four (16.4 million women) and as you will discover later in this book, a good number of those women will be experiencing menopause symptoms.

According to one UK study reported by Suban Abdulla in Yahoo Finance, "over half of working women aged forty to sixty-five have experienced three or more symptoms they know, or believe, are related to menopause, including hot flashes (forty-seven percent), night sweats (forty-one percent) and feeling tired (thirty-five percent). Half of all women experiencing three or more symptoms have experienced at least one further detrimental impact on their working lives including, a negative impact on their relationships with colleagues, having to reduce their working hours, or considering resigning. Only twelve percent of the respondents said they have not experienced menopausal symptoms."[10] Thus, eighty-eight percent of that huge number of women are affected by the symptoms of menopause.

Businesses frequently offer programs for smoking cessation, pregnancy, pregnancy lactation, weight loss, insomnia, and others. These are important wellness programs. But none of those conditions happens to every woman. In contrast, menopause happens to every woman who lives long enough. Yet fewer than ten percent of UK businesses provide employees any information about menopause.[11] The UK is much more progressive about menopause in the workplace than the United States where only about one percent of businesses provide any information about menopause to their employees. Menopause in the workplace is almost universally viewed as a taboo topic—something unspoken, and often treated as a joke.

Why isn't more being done to help these women?

It's a question we are often asked when invited to speak to women's groups, companies, and women's organizations. It seems companies are either unaware of, or ignoring the need and the impact that menopause plays on their workforce. Studies clearly show that addressing menopause symptoms in the workplace has the potential to improve absenteeism, employee retention, and productivity while at the same time causing women to feel more positive about their company.[12] It can also save companies millions of dollars, and society billions of dollars in direct and indirect costs.

We know this to be true from our own first-hand experiences. After treating over ten thousand patients, one of us (MS) has heard hundreds of stories from women trying desperately to cope with their menopause experience at work, while the other (SS) is a previvor who was thrown into early menopause due to surgery for cancer prevention and realized first-hand how impactful being thrown into menopause can be. However, the final decision to write this book happened when I (MS) was contacted by a phone call from Allyson Chiu of the Washington Post asking for a comment on a podcast by former First Lady Michelle Obama.[13] In the podcast, Ms. Obama shared some of the challenges she has faced with her own hot flashes, and how they were affecting her work. She recounted what it was like to arrive at a presentation she was about to give and suddenly being confronted with a wave of hot flashes:

> I'm dressed, I need to get out, walk into an event, and literally it was like somebody put a furnace in my core, and turned it on high, and then everything started melting, the fifty-six-year-old year old former First Lady recounted during an episode of her new eponymous Spotify podcast.[14]

In one brief, candid comment that followed, Michelle Obama voiced what millions of other women are experiencing in the workplace every day when she shared her thought, "This is crazy, I can't, I can't, I can't do this." And then she said,

> What a woman's body is taking her through is important information. It's an important thing to take up space in a society, because half of us are going through this, but we're living like it's not happening.[14]

When Michelle Obama is talking about the experience of her menopause symptoms and how it's affecting her work in a podcast, and how we're living like it's not happening, it's time to shine a spotlight on the unmet needs, lack of awareness, and limited understanding surrounding menopause at work. This is not only for women, but also for their co-workers, and their employers. This can normalize a natural transition that happens to every woman who lives long enough, and highlight things that can be done medically, personally, and programmatically in the workplace, and to offer resources and suggestions to improve this large, and largely ignored and growing reality.

Menopause is happening at a rate of six thousand more women every day in the US alone. That's nearly 2.2 million women per year. Women in the workplace, employers, HR, and every link in the workforce chain needs to be aware that menopause is happening, and it is having an impact that needs to be acknowledged, addressed, and its negative impact eliminated.

Menopause is just another part of life, like pregnancy, which almost every workplace acknowledges and for which it has policies and procedures in place. The difference is, pregnancy doesn't happen to every woman—menopause does.

Women are able to achieve so much with only a small percentage having their menopause symptoms addressed. Imagine what the positive impact will be when they are able to work unencumbered.

Bottom Line: Menopause is a silent ceiling, something that is happening universally but getting little or no attention. It is affecting nearly a quarter of the workforce across the globe. Addressing the menopause experience at work will allow women at the peak of their careers to flourish and continue to make significant contributions. The impact of not addressing the menopause experience is an increased potential loss of women from the workforce, absenteeism, and less than possible performance. With more information and support for both women and the workplace, and by normalizing menopause, much of these negative effects can be improved or resolved.

CHAPTER 3

Menopause 101

A study says owning a dog makes you ten years younger. My first thought was to rescue two more, but I don't want to go through menopause again.

– **Joan Rivers**

How much do you know about menopause?

If you are like most people, including many healthcare providers and a whole lot of women, your understanding of menopause may need some brushing up. There are a lot of myths, misunderstandings, misconceptions and misinformation surrounding this topic.

It starts with little girls. Moms often have "the talk" with their daughters about their first period, but very few girls are given "the talk" about their last menstrual period. Menopause has never been a part of health education in schools until literally just now. In the UK, the National Health Service (NHS) is adding menopause education to the sexual health curriculum for schools so girls will realize what is happening to their bodies when menopause symptoms begin.[15] Adding menopause to school's curriculum will help to normalize it and help women recognize it. We believe US schools should follow suit.

What does menopause mean to you?

If you're not sure how to answer this question, or if the first things that come to mind are old wives tales you heard from your mother or grandmother, don't worry. We'll explain the basics so that it will all make sense.

The medical definition of menopause is twelve consecutive months of not having a period. You can also go through menopause from removal of the ovaries, radiation, or some other medical intervention. All women who live long enough experience menopause, It's natural and it's universal. However, according to a study done by Drs. Avis and Crawford, "cross-cultural studies find that women's menopausal experiences are far from universal, in fact, evidence shows that menopause is strongly shaped by social and cultural factors. The symptoms women experience, the meaning of menopause, their attitudes towards menopause, and whether or not they seek treatment all vary across cultures."[16]

How a woman transitions through this normal life experience has a lot to do with her background and culture, which is intertwined with diet, lifestyle, societal norms, and environment. Because the workplace includes all of those elements and is a place where women spend considerable time, logically it also impacts a woman's menopausal experience.

What happens biologically during menopause?

Menopause literally means the stopping of menses – menses pause. Though the mean age is fifty-one years, as the table below shows, menopause also happens among women in their forties, thirties, and even in their twenties.

Before age 20 (Premature Menopause)	1 out of 10,000 women
Before age 30 (Premature Menopause)	1 out of 1,000 women
Before age forty (Premature Menopause)	1 out of 100 women
Before age forty-five (Early Menopause)	1 out of 10-20 women

Compiled by Mache Seibel, MD for The Estrogen Window[17]

Just like the caterpillar and butterfly, menopause is part of an ongoing continuum of life: prepuberty, puberty, reproduction, perimenopause, menopause, and post-menopause.

A number of years ago, several major medical organizations tried to organize the timeline leading to menopause and tie it to the most common menopausal symptoms and testing. When they tried to organize their findings by age, nothing made any sense.

However, when they used the last or final menstrual period (FMP) as a reference point for the one thing all women have in common, everything fell into place. They called it the Stages of Reproductive Aging Workshop or STRAW. Ten years later they refined their findings to include certain blood tests and other criteria and called it STRAW+10.[18] The image below is a summary of those findings.

| Menarche | | | | | | | FMP (0) | | | |

Stage	-5	-4	-3b	-3a	-2	-1	+1a	+1b	+1c	+2
Terminology	REPRODUCTIVE				MENOPAUSAL TRANSITION		POSTMENOPAUSE			
	Early	Peak	Late		Early	Late	Early			Late
					Perimenopause					
Duration	variable				variable	1-3 years	2 years (1+1)		3-6 years	Remaining lifespan
PRINCIPAL CRITERIA										
Menstrual Cycle	Variable to regular	Regular	Regular	Subtle changes in Flow/ Length	Variable Length Persistent ≥7- day difference in length of consecutive cycles	Interval of amenorrhea of >=60 days				
SUPPORTIVE CRITERIA										
Endocrine FSH AMH Inhibin B			Normal Low Low	Variable* Low Low	↑ Variable* Low Low	↑ >25 IU/L** Low Low	↑ Variable* Low Low	Stabilizes Very Low Very Low		
Antral Follicle Count 2-10 mm			Low	Low	Low	Low	Very Low	Very Low		
DESCRIPTIVE CHARACTERISTICS										
Symptoms						Vasomotor symptoms Likely	Vasomotor symptoms Most Likely			Increasing symptoms of urogenital atrophy

* Blood draw on cycle days 2-5   ↑ = elevated
**Approximate expected level based on assays using current pituitary standard[87-89]

Straw+10 Executive Summary (2011) was sponsored by the American Society for Reproductive Medicine, the National Institutes on Aging, the National Institute of Child Health and Human Development, and the North American Menopause Society. It was compiled by people from five countries and applies regardless of women's age, ethnicity, body size or lifestyle characteristics.[18]

At first glance this table is a bit confusing, but if you look at it carefully, a woman or her healthcare provider can figure out where she is in her menopausal transition. The seemingly random information is grouped into stages so that the focus is less about age and more about the physical and hormonal transition that is happening. Remember, menopause is about transition, not age, and being able to gauge where you are can be very helpful.

Here's a quick explanation of the various medical terms used in STRAW+10 to help you interpret the table:

- **FSH (follicle stimulating hormone)** – FSH is a hormone in the pituitary gland that stimulates dormant eggs in the ovary to begin to mature. As it matures, each egg forms a fluid filled sac around itself and the egg (called an oocyte) with its surrounding fluid is called a follicle.
- **AMH or anti Mullerian Hormone** – When a woman is born, each ovary has a basket of eggs that reduce in number as she gets older. The cells around each egg produce a hormone called AMH. As the number of eggs gets smaller, so does the AMH level. AMH levels are used by fertility doctors to get a rough estimate of a woman's fertility, and menopause doctors use AMH for a rough estimate of how far a woman is from menopause.
- **Inhibin B** – Inhibin B is a protein produced by the cells that surround each egg. As a woman gets closer to menopause, the levels of Inhibin B get lower and lower.
- **Antral Follicles** – The fluid filled sac around each developing egg is called an antral follicle. As a woman gets closer to menopause, the number of antral follicles gets less and less. These can be measured by pelvic ultrasound.

The Symptoms of Menopause

Remember puberty? Raging hormones, skin changes, body changes, menstrual changes, mood changes—change, change, change. At the end of puberty, most women enter a window of relative hormonal balance for roughly thirty-five years unless interrupted by pregnancy. The major hormones, estrogen and progesterone, are synchronized, mood is much more constant unless you struggle with premenstrual syndrome (PMS), and periods are fairly regular. Then comes perimenopause and bam, things start to get very different. As one woman told me, "When I asked for a smoking hot body, menopause was not what I had in mind."

If you think about menopause hormonally, it's kind of like puberty... only backwards. The perfectly balanced hormones become increasingly unbalanced. And that impacts just about every cell in your body. Those hormonal imbalances are what cause the symptoms of menopause.

The good news is that most women get only some of the symptoms, and up to a quarter of women get few or no bothersome symptoms. Let's alphabetically look at what can happen from head to toe...

Common Perimenopause Symptoms

Acne	Forgetfulness	Joint pain
Anxiety	Frequent urination	Loss of libido
Bloating	Hair loss or thinning	Mood swings
Breast tenderness	Headaches	Night sweats
Crying	Hot flashes	Heart palpitations
Decreased libido	Interrupted sleep	Urinary incontinence
Depression	Irregular periods	Vaginal dryness/pain
Facial hair	Irritability	Weight gain in middle

Having any or many of these symptoms would be bad enough at any time, but it's especially challenging when the symptoms follow you to work. Imagine having to work with the additional burden of foggy thinking, hot flashes, sensitive bladder, irritability and more. To discover how your perimenopause experience compares to other women, take this free two-minute quiz at MenopauseQuiz.com.[19]

"What is happening to my body and my brain?"

Are you a woman who is used to juggling work, social, and family obligations and who once slept through the night and managed your days? Now, do you suddenly find yourself waking up at 4:00 a.m. with heart palpitations or feeling sleepy, anxious, or teary during the day? Do you sometimes lose focus and have a shorter fuse than you used to? Throw in a few mood swings, headaches, and forgetting where the car is parked and you begin to wonder if something is physically or mentally wrong with you. Are you hot one minute and peeling off layers of clothing, then cold the next and putting on a sweater, chilled? Do you feel anxious and a little depressed? Your brain is a bit foggy and your mind doesn't seem as sharp as it once was. All your pants are suddenly feeling a size too small. You have heart palpitations and worry you have a heart problem. Your mojo is a no show. Your vagina feels as dry as the Sahara. You urinate more frequently than you used to.

If you are forty-five to fifty-five years old, give or take a few years, there's probably nothing "wrong" with you. Your body is transitioning toward menopause.

Menopause can take place in one of the three following ways:

1. **Natural or spontaneous menopause:** When a woman's ovaries naturally stop making enough estrogen to produce a menstrual cycle. This is what the STRAW+10 is summarizing and is the most common form of menopause.

2. **Surgical menopause:** When a woman's ovaries are removed by surgery prior to natural menopause. The woman is in menopause from the time the ovaries are removed. If the ovaries are removed before age forty-five, the woman is in early menopause. Having a hysterectomy (his-tuh-RECK-tuh-me) (surgical removal of the uterus) will stop menstruation, but it does not cause menopause unless both ovaries are removed, which is called a bilateral oophorectomy (oo-for-RECK-tuh-me). It is important to know that if you have a hysterectomy, even if your ovaries are left in, you will most likely lose some of the ovaries' hormone-producing ability within the

first few years after surgery. Within the first six months after surgery, twenty-five percent of people lose ovarian function and within three years, forty percent lose ovarian function. The average time an ovary continues to function after hysterectomy is seven years.

Each year, about 600,000 hysterectomies are performed in the United States. It's important to be aware of how a hysterectomy could affect your hormones if you are one of these women.

3. **Induced or iatrogenic menopause:** When a woman's ovaries cease to function due to radiation treatments, chemotherapy, or some other drug, pronounced eye-at-rho-JEN-ik.

How Long Will These Menopausal Symptoms Last?

"I'm sixty-five. Why am I still getting occasional hot flashes and regular night sweats?" Repeated studies have found that hot flashes sputter out for most women after three to five years in menopause, but some continue to have symptoms, generally not as severe, for ten years or more. About one-third of women who take estrogen find that some of the symptoms of menopause return once they stop or as they taper off their treatment. Approximately fifteen percent of women have hot flashes at ages fifty-five to fifty-nine, and 6.5 percent continue to have hot flashes up to age sixty-five.

We are beginning to understand the mechanism for hot flashes, night sweats, and some of the other symptoms of menopause. What we know for sure is that low estrogen levels are the cause. The part of the brain that regulates temperature—the body's thermostat—isn't working properly. New non-hormonal medications are being developed for hot flashes that work through receptors in that part of the brain. If you're experiencing hot flashes and night sweats, cutting out caffeine, alcohol, and spicy foods can help. That includes chocolate which has caffeine.

By the time perimenopausal patients speak with me, they have usually already been to at least one other doctor, often an internist or a general practitioner. But some have been to a cardiologist, a psychiatrist, a neurologist, a urologist, or all of the above. Even gynecologists sometimes miss the diagnosis.

Many women are put through a battery of costly tests and multiple doctor visits that come back negative. In an effort to help, doctors often prescribe antidepressants or sleeping pills for anxiety or sleeplessness. They get EKGs to see if there may be a heart problem, instead of determining that the palpitations are perimenopause related. If you are experiencing the symptoms described in this chapter, talk with your gynecologist or other healthcare provider familiar with perimenopause and menopause. Don't suffer in silence. Treatments for every symptom are available, so ask. Also know that even though your estrogen levels are dropping during perimenopause, you can still become pregnant. Unless you want to get pregnant, be sure to use a reliable method of birth control until you have gone twelve months without a period. Many women choose to use a diaphragm, condoms, or an IUD in perimenopause. Every year or so one of my patients comes in with a "surprise" pregnancy. As Yogi Berra said, "It ain't over till it's over."

Menopausal symptoms can have a profound effect on how a woman feels both physically and emotionally, eroding self-confidence and even leaving many questioning if they are losing their minds. In fact, many women confide that the memory issues surrounding menopause have them worried they are developing dementia. They are not, but all of this can affect workability. Imagine how helpful it would be if menopause education and support was routinely included in workplace wellness programs. Imagine if managers and co-workers all understood what you were going through and that it was challenging and normal.

Bottom Line: Menopause is the transition from reproduction into post-reproduction. It's a lot like puberty, only backwards. It begins with hormone imbalance and eventually results in very low levels of estrogen. Hormonal imbalance leads to mood swings, anxiety, sensitive bladder, irregular periods, and more. Menopause can happen at any age, and the symptoms can last from a few years to more than a decade. If a woman enters menopause before age forty and has not completed childbearing, she will face the additional burden of infertility if she still desires children. The good news is that there are treatments for all of the symptoms and conditions. In the meantime, the menopause experience can create real challenges personally, in relationships, and at work.

CHAPTER 4

Estrogen, Menopause and You

I love the smell of estrogen in the morning.

– Katie Couric

Why a Chapter on Estrogen?

You may be wondering why there is a chapter on estrogen in a book on the impact of menopause on women in the workplace. The answer is really very simple. Estrogen, sometimes referred to as HRT (hormone replacement therapy) or HT (hormone therapy), is arguably the most effective treatment for the symptoms of menopause. Yet nine out of ten women choose not to take it. The goal of this book is not to explain why taking estrogen is both safe and effective for the vast majority of women. You can read about in the best-selling book, *The Estrogen Fix.*[20]

The reason that we're discussing estrogen in this book is because as a result of estrogen phobia, the vast majority of women have chosen to tough it out rather than figure it out and get the support and treatment they need to feel their best during menopause and beyond. American poet Sonya Sones wrote a parody on Hamlet's "To be or not to be…" soliloquy to put the dilemma into perspective:

To take estrogen or not to take estrogen:
That is the question.
Whether 'tis nobler to abstain and suffer
The sweat and puddles of outrageous flashes
Or to take arms against a sea of mood swings,
And by opposing end them? To die: to sleep,
No more, at first the studies say 'twill end
The heart attacks and thousand bouts of bloat
That flesh is heir to, 'tis a true confusion –
For then they say 'twill cause us all to die
Perchance from breast cancer, ay, there's the rub,
For who can dream or even sleep while worrying about
What doctors might be saying come next week?

Sonya Sones

Fear of estrogen is so great, it has tainted even non-hormonal menopause treatments, resulting in many women not seeking treatment of any kind. That decision has had a huge impact on women in general and in the workplace, because although estrogen is the most effective treatment for most menopause symptoms, non-hormonal treatment for menopause symptoms has also been shown to improve workability.[21] Daysal and Orsini (2014) studied the number of women leaving the labor force due to the symptoms of menopause.[22] They concluded that those discontinuing HRT following the Women's Health Initiative (WHI), a landmark 2002 study that erroneously reported taking estrogen increased the risk of breast cancer, heart disease, strokes and other health issues, were thirty percent more likely to leave their jobs than those who continued to take the medication.[23] The WHI had a huge impact on women in the workplace. That is why we are addressing estrogen and menopause briefly, to clear up some of the myths that surround this medication. Here is a short version of how things got so confusing for today's working woman.

Framing the WHI

The date was July 9, 2002. I was seeing patients in my office just outside Boston, and the phones started ringing off the hook. The receptionists couldn't keep up with all the panic-stricken patients frantic to get an opinion on that day's headline, "Hormone Replacement Study a Shock to the Medical System." You would literally have had to be on the moon not to have heard about that and related headlines. The panic was due to the initial report of a study called the Women's Health Initiative study, or WHI, for short.[23] It was to be the study that proved once and for all that taking either an estrogen called Premarin, with or without a synthetic progesterone called Provera, was safe.

The first WHI study assessed the risks and benefits of women who had not had a hysterectomy and were taking a combo pill called Prempro. Each pill contained a specific dosage of the estrogen Premarin plus the synthetic progesterone (also called a progestin) named Provera (hence the name Prempro). The WHI was halted prematurely because Prempro reportedly caused a significantly increased risk of breast cancer, heart attacks, blood clots, and strokes. It's easy to see how scary this would be to every woman taking any form of estrogen, with or without a progestin. And we're talking about tens of millions of women. In fact, at the time of that study's release, estrogen was the most prescribed medication on the planet.

When the news broke about the potential risks of Prempro, eighty percent of women taking any form of estrogen, and that was millions of women, threw away their hormones that same day. What followed was a medical tsunami. Women and their doctors felt anger, fear, distrust, a lack of answers...the women also felt a lot of hot flashes, brain fog, anxiety, and suffering.

How The WHI Got It Wrong

Prior to the WHI study, the benefits of estrogen were thought to be so strong that millions and millions of women were given a prescription for it. These earlier studies were all observational, meaning women who entered menopause were given estrogen and then their symptoms were observed and reported. Unfortunately, there had never been a large study that compared estrogen alone or estrogen plus progestin to a placebo pill. That was the purpose of the WHI study—to finally have a gold standard double-blind placebo-controlled study about estrogen that scientists could talk about in which a monitoring group not involved in the study randomly assigns patients to one group or the other, and keeps track of the group assignments and results during the trial.

WHI Study Design

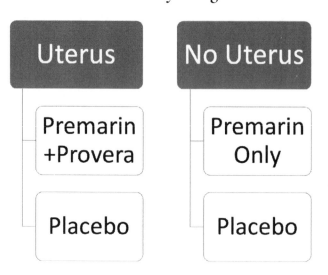

Premarin was by far the most widely prescribed estrogen in the world. Women in menopause who have a uterus (have not had a hysterectomy) and who take Premarin (or any estrogen) must also take either progesterone or a synthetic progesterone. The need for progesterone or a progestin stems from the fact that Premarin (or any estrogen) taken alone causes the uterine lining to grow. That is its purpose. Progesterone causes the uterine lining to stop growing and compact so it is the perfect place for an embryo to implant. After a decade or more of taking Premarin alone, the continued uterine lining growth will cause some women to develop either precancer or cancer of the uterine lining (endometrial cancer).

By taking either progesterone or a progestin along with estrogen, abnormal uterine lining changes are virtually non-existent. When the WHI study began, no oral form of progesterone was available, so the study used a synthetic progestin called Provera (generic name: medroxyprogesterone acetate). Provera was by far the most common progestin in use at that time. We have bioidentical (same chemical structure as the body makes) progesterone available today so women don't have to take synthetic progesterone if they don't want to. The tens of thousands of women enrolled into the study were supposed to be healthy and range in age from fifty to seventy-nine. However, early on the study ran into a really huge problem that ultimately led to the study coming to inaccurate conclusions. Many women were already taking estrogen— the researchers had difficulty finding enough untreated women in their fifties to enroll into the study. Why? Because women usually begin taking estrogen in their fifties when the symptoms of menopause are typically most bothersome. Most of the women in their fifties who might be interested in taking estrogen were already taking it. The study had to enroll a skewed percentage of women in their sixties and seventies into the study to take estrogen. Instead of the study enrolling an equal number of women in their fifties, sixties and seventies, seventy-five percent of the women in the WHI study who were given estrogen or estrogen plus progestin were in their sixties and seventies (the mean age of the hormone treated women was sixty-three). In the placebo group, seventy-five percent of the women were in their fifties. That flaw resulted in the WHI study comparing women mostly in their sixties and seventies taking a hormone to women in their fifties taking a placebo. That is a very big flaw.

In addition, the study was supposed to include only healthy women. Since they needed to enroll more women, they allowed women into the study who were smokers, had diabetes, high blood pressure, and were overweight. Those are all risk factors for both cancer and heart disease.

When you stop to think about it, who do you think would have more cancer and heart disease—women in their sixties and seventies who were smokers, had diabetes, high blood pressure or were overweight, or healthy women in their fifties? If you guessed the older age group, you guessed right. That design flaw caused the results of the study findings to be completely incorrect. That is why later studies found such different results. Well over a decade later, the same women from the WHI study were matched up by comparable age groups instead of lumping them all into one Prempro or Premarin only group.[24] That changed everything. By comparing comparably aged women who either took a hormone or took a placebo, almost all of the negative findings went away. In fact, the follow up studies found that beginning estrogen, or estrogen plus progestin, while a woman was still in her fifties, or within ten years of starting menopause, was both safe and effective for most women.

Here is one more fact from the follow up studies that you should know. When the WHI study was reevaluated eighteen years after it was published with the women matched by comparable ages, the women who took either estrogen, or estrogen and progestin, in the original WHI studies lived on average two years longer than the women who took a placebo.[25]

Estrogen only is safer than placebo for women without a uterus

In 2004, a second WHI report was published that evaluated the risks and benefits of Premarin alone in women who had a hysterectomy. Because they did not have a uterus, they didn't need Provera to protect the uterine lining. The results were strikingly different. The 2004 WHI study, found that Premarin taken alone did not cause an increased risk of breast cancer and might actually decrease breast cancer risk.[26] Premarin alone also didn't increase the risk of heart disease. But the damage to estrogen's safety was done and its reputation already destroyed.

Another large study of hormone therapy, the Danish Osteoporosis Prevention Study (DOPS) also reported favorable results about estrogen only:

> After ten years of randomized treatment, women receiving hormone replacement therapy early after menopause had a significantly reduced risk of mortality, heart failure, or myocardial infarction, without any apparent increase in risk of cancer, venous thromboembolism, or stroke.[27]

Their results were confirmed in 2020, when a long-term follow-up of the same women from the original WHI study[28] found that women who took estrogen-only had lower rates of breast cancer than women who did not, and lower rates of colon cancer, osteoporosis[29] (bone thinning that increases the risk of a broken bone), heart disease,[30] and diabetes. According to an article in Forbes[31] magazine from a yet-unpublished preprint,[32] NIH Doctors Seo Baik and Clement McDonald reviewed 1.5 million women's records from the Medicare database to determine whether or not taking estrogen-only therapy increased the risk of cancer, heart disease, and death. Their findings showed that "estrogen-only led to a twenty-one percent reduction in the risk of death, and a similar reduction in the risk of breast cancer, endometrial cancer, and ovarian cancer." In contrast, taking a combination of estrogen plus progestin led to an increased risk of breast cancer. We know from the follow-up WHI study that the increased risk is not more than 0.001 percent, i.e., not more than one additional case of breast cancer per one thousand women who take the medication. Most menopause experts feel that is a reasonable risk given the many benefits.

The message now seems clear...

The compromised study design and resulting news coverage of the initial Women's Health Initiative in 2002 provided inaccurate and misleading information. Follow-up studies using the same data, but adjusted for when estrogen was begun i.e. the age when women began estrogen, clearly prove that taking estrogen is safe and effective for the majority of women. This is particularly true if women begin estrogen in their estrogen window—within ten years of beginning menopause or before age sixty.[33]

The Impact of the WHI

Negative misinformation about estrogen is responsible for a new perspective to the menopause experience. "My symptoms are making me feel uncomfortable, embarrassed, miserable, tired, foggy, less interested in sex, less effective at work, gain weight, or incredibly moody, (you fill in the blank), but they won't last forever. I can tough it out." That indirect and unfortunate outcome from the confusion caused by the WHI caused the vast majority of a generation of women to make a conscious decision to avoid estrogen. A subset of those women also chose to avoid estrogen alternatives. All of them are "toughing it out." So millions are unnecessarily suffering through perimenopause and menopause.

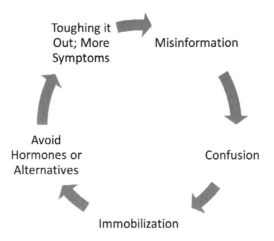

How do you feel about estrogen?

Are you convinced that whatever the benefits, no matter how great, it isn't worth the risk and worry of taking it?

If so, reevaluate your mind-set. The current way of thinking created a brain drain for women—two decades of women enduring menopausal side effects that could have been avoided and that, as you will discover, has robbed millions of women of quality of life and advancement at work. In addition, emerging research is strongly suggesting that the lower levels of estrogen found at menopause increases a woman's risk for the COVID-19 virus.[34] That is why being informed is so important.

Bottom Line: If you are having menopause symptoms, there is zero need for you to go untreated and suffer in silence. This includes natural, surgical or induced menopause, and early or premature menopause. Estrogen is safe and effective for most women. However, if you can't or don't want to take estrogen, that's OK. There are non-estrogen treatments, knowledgeable doctors and coaches to guide you, and lifestyle changes that can make a difference. Women undergoing cancer treatment or cancer survivors face additional challenges, but symptomatic treatments are available. Those who are transgender may also face additional menopausal challenges and should seek treatment. Treating your menopause symptoms could save your quality of life, your health, your job, your marriage.

Imagine how much better and how much more empowered you will feel. Do not tough it out, figure it out. That will change everything.

CHAPTER 5

The Impact of Menopause on Women at Work

It is increasingly clear to me, since I became perimenopausal, that we do not have nearly enough conversations about how this monumental life event, the menopause, affects our working habits.

Adah Parris, Chair of Mental Health First Aid (MHFA) England

When you read through the following list of physical and psychological symptoms described by Brewis, et. al. in Table 6,[35] try to imagine what it would feel like if you were meeting with your boss, running a meeting, or just talking with coworkers and you were dealing with one or more of these symptoms...

Physical Symptoms: Dizziness or faintness, head tightness/pressure, numbness, loss of feeling in hands and feet, headaches, muscle and joint pain, difficulty breathing, hot flashes, night sweats, sweating, heart palpitations (being very aware of heart beat, heart racing or skipping, tightness in chest), sleep problems (difficulty falling or staying asleep, waking early) and muscle and joint problems. Irregular periods and/or very heavy blood flow, weight gain or weight redistribution, aching limbs, swollen ankles, sore or tender breasts, pins and needles, dry or itchy skin, skin color changes, thinning, dry or itchy hair, growth or loss of body hair, growth of facial hair, bladder infections, loss of bone density, clumsiness.[35]

Psychological Symptoms: Heart racing or beating strongly, tension or nervousness, sleeping difficulties, being excitable, anxiety or panic attacks, concentration problems, fatigue or loss of energy, loss of interest in most things, unhappiness or depression, crying spells, feeling irritable. Depressive mood (feeling sad, tearful or down, lacking drive, mood swings), irritability (feeling tense, nervous or aggressive), anxiety (restlessness, feeling panicky), physical and mental exhaustion (lower performance, memory difficulties, concentration problems, forgetfulness).

Who could function at peak performance with these symptoms vying for your attention? It sure wouldn't be easy.[35]

Believe it or not, this is not all of the symptoms found in scientific studies about the impact of menopause on women's economic participation in the workplace.[35] With so many symptoms, how could menopause not impact women at work? Growing evidence proves that it does. According to the United States Bureau of Labor Statistics, as a group, women ages forty-five to fifty-four and women fifty-five and over are among the fastest growing groups in the workforce.[36] Each day over six thousand women enter menopause. In the UK, women over the age of fifty are the fastest growing group in the workforce. The billion-dollar question is, "Why doesn't the United States address women's menopause experience at work?!" Menopause in the workplace has started to be addressed in other countries like Great Britain, Australia and Japan, but the United States is far behind these other countries. It's time to get the ball rolling to help both the women and the businesses.

Data show that the physical and psychological symptoms of menopause can have such an impact on wellbeing that in the UK, one in four women have considered leaving their jobs because of it, and millions of women have exited the workforce due to their menopause experience.[37] In a UK study conducted by CIPD (The Chartered Institute of Personnel Development), which is the main professional body to accredit and award professional human resources (HR) qualifications, three out of five (fifty-nine percent) working women between the ages of forty-five and fifty-five who are experiencing menopause symptoms at work say it has a negative impact on them. Of those women experiencing symptoms:

- Nearly two-thirds (sixty-five percent) said they were less able to concentrate
- More than half (fifty-eight percent) said they experience more stress
- More than half (fifty-two percent) said they felt less patient with clients and colleagues.[38]

In a 2021 Japanese study published in the journal Menopause, researchers confirmed what most working women in menopause already know—the higher the number of symptoms, the more their work performance is affected.[39] Before you despair, there is good news: menopause symptoms are all treatable, and adjusting workplace accommodations can help as well.

How Does Menopause Affect Women At Work?

An increasing number of studies and surveys, mostly outside of the United States, offer a window into the diverse impact of the menopause experience on work.[40, 41, 42] That experience is influenced not only by menopausal symptoms and context, but also by the physical and psychosocial characteristics of the workplace environment.[43]

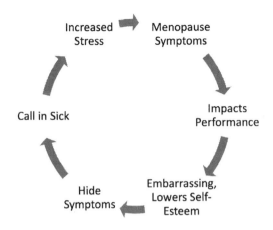

A 2021 article by Maria Evandrou, et al in the journal Maturitas reported that 53.5 percent of employed women at age fifty reported at least one severe menopausal symptom.[44] A key finding was that women experiencing severe menopausal symptoms had a higher chance of either leaving work or reducing their hours. Factors that influenced the women's decision were greatly influenced by whether or not they used hormone therapy and how much money their partner earned. In some instances the stress of work contributes to the symptoms, in others it is the physical working environment that increases the intensity of symptoms.[45] One little-talked about side effect of intense symptoms is that they increase a woman's risk for becoming dehydrated, which can further affect her work experience.[46] Easy access to cold water is a real plus for the workplace.

The work environment can also affect a woman's perception of her symptoms and her self-esteem. Imagine being in a meeting and finding your menopause status being outed by a severe and long-lasting hot flash.[47] It can feel like at any second, everyone will know you are one of those women. It is also possible that one woman could experience a hot flash that causes her to appear visibly flushed, while another could sit quietly in a meeting with no outward signs, but feeling the same as her counterpart. These types of experiences cause women to keep their symptoms private, and a lack of privacy in companies causes women to hide their symptoms.

When symptoms become too severe, many women call in sick. If they require a doctor's appointment, they make up excuses for the appointment so no one will know what is really troubling them. In one report, nearly one third (thirty percent) said they had taken sick leave due to their symptoms, but only a quarter (twenty-five percent) felt able to tell their managers the real reason they were absent due to privacy issues, embarrassment or because their manager was unsupportive.[38]

Since the WHI was reported in 2002, there has been a steep decline in the use of estrogen containing products to treat hot flashes. And even though there are alternative treatment options, coaching, as well as lifestyle changes, seventy percent of women with moderate to severe hot flashes remain untreated.[48] That leaves millions of menopausal women trying to perform at their best while struggling with sometimes debilitating symptoms. The workplace must normalize the menopause experience and educate women and their managers about menopause to remove the stigma associated with it.

Things at work that make coping with hot flashes more difficult

WORK SITUATIONS	MORE DIFFICULT (percent)
Hot/unventilated offices/workspaces	71.3
Formal meetings	62.8
High visibility work (e.g. presentations)	45.2
Learning new things/procedures	42.8
Tasks requiring attention to detail	36.4
Shared offices/workspaces	34.9

Griffiths A, et al: Menopause at work: An electronic survey of employees' attitudes in the UK. Maturitas 76 (2013) 155-159.[49]

As you can see in the table above, the more stressful the task or situation, or the more unventilated the workspace, the more difficult it is for a woman to cope with her symptoms, particularly if her symptoms are not being treated. Once you understand this, it's easy to see why addressing those symptoms impacts a woman's performance at work and her decision to continue working. This concept has become so clear that researchers in the UK have called for menopause to be considered as a work, health, and safety (WHS) issue in an effort to retain female workers by supporting them through the menopause transition.[50] Here are some of the documented ways menopause symptoms can impact women and indirectly, the businesses that employ them:

- Decreased work productivity
- Absenteeism/Presenteeism
- Loss of confidence
- Increased desire to reduce hours or drop out of the workforce
- Lower self esteem
- Increased sick leave
- Impaired performance
- Reduced work capacity[51,52]

An opinion piece in the *Washington Post* entitled "Is Menopause Really Driving Women Out Of The Workforce?" found that menopause symptoms can impact both job performance and attitudes toward work.[52] Another survey by Working Mother Media and Pfizer found that forty-eight percent of women believed their symptoms made their work life more difficult, and one in five altered their schedule over it.[52,53] A 2020 study found that the more issues women experienced with menopause, the more their job performance suffered.[54]

Why Women Need Support in Menopause

Menopause is experienced differently by individual women and by different cultures. A fortunate few will not experience any or few symptoms. But for roughly eighty percent of women, their menopause experience will affect their quality of life, and for one third of those women, the symptoms will be distressful and escalate something as natural as menopausal body changes into a disruptive experience with far reaching and impactful work implications. According to the Advisory, Conciliation and Arbitration Service (ACAS), an independent public body in the UK that works with millions of employers and employees every year to improve workplace relationships, it is increasingly likely that the effects of the menopause can cause them to:

- Feel ill
- Lose confidence to do their job
- Suffer from stress, anxiety and depression
- Leave their job[55]

Even in work environments as diverse as policing, a study commissioned by the British Association of Women in Policing found that some women police officers reported that the tiredness and insomnia they associated with menopausal transition affected their capacity to function normally at work.[56] In the current work environment, more than nine out of ten UK workplaces do not have a policy for menopause. That percentage drops to less than one percent in the United States. The workplace is often unaware of the impact menopause is having on their C-suite executives, colleagues, or support staff who are silently dealing with the experience of menopause while also contending with the stresses of life at home as well as at work.

Why many female workers do not reveal their menopause experience

Most companies are unaware that many if not most workers do not disclose their menopausal experience at work. A study in The Guardian reported, "Although it directly affects half the population, it has remained a stubbornly taboo topic." This occurs in part because employers provide no support for it, and in part because women fear being stigmatized and ridiculed for it. Menopause must be a bad thing, why else would no one be talking about it. The Guardian article goes on to report, "Women shared that the lack of discussion about the menopause meant that they had been unprepared for the experience."[57] These two ever present facts result in many of the women who require time off from work because of their menopause experience not telling their employer the real reasons for their absence. Why would women lie and keep a medical issue that affects half the population a secret? According to the ACAS, it is because the worker feels: their symptoms are a private and/or personal matter, their symptoms might embarrass them, and/or the person they confide in, they do not know their line manager well enough, or because their line manager is a man, or younger, or unsympathetic.

There are also darker worries that women fear:

- their symptoms will not be taken seriously
- if they do talk, their symptoms will become widely known at work
- they will be thought to be less capable
- their job security and/or chances of promotion will be harmed[58]

Think about it. If the word on the street is that talking about menopause is taboo, who would want to let it be known that you are one of "those women" with one of "those symptoms" which meant one of "those darker fears" were going to become a reality. If the overwhelming majority of businesses have no menopause policy in place, women have little recourse when their needs aren't met.

Consider this scenario. You're in your mid-forties plus or minus. Up until now you've been very successful at juggling your life, relationships, work and community activities. You start feeling tired, anxious, foggy, don't feel well, and call in sick. You're more irritable at home and work, warm and sweaty, and your life feels like it's spiraling out of control. You take time off from work to talk with a doctor about your mood and motivation. A few months, later you take off another half day to talk with a different doctor about your sleep. Now you're noticing your bladder is more sensitive so you have to keep leaving meetings to go to the bathroom which is across the building. Your genitourinary syndrome of menopause also includes vaginal dryness and your partner is concerned because you're less interested in sex and at the same time is also anxious about causing discomfort. You don't know what's happening to your body, but it isn't good, and you feel out of control.

If menopause and perimenopause continue to be swept under the rug, if your work environment has no policy around menopause, if you believe that talking about menopause at work is taboo, that creates a very awkward situation that can negatively impact self-esteem.

You contrive an excuse to take time off from work to talk with a doctor about your symptoms so you can discover what can be done to help you feel better personally, at work, and in your relationship. And if your healthcare provider isn't current or comfortable discussing your symptoms, you end up feeling embarrassed that you ever asked about it.

All too many women are told "it's all normal at this age," so get over it. Many are incorrectly told there is no safe and effective treatment, or they are given contradictory advice on hormone replacement therapy. It's even more difficult if you are a cancer survivor. Many cancer epidemiologists believe there is an increased risk of breast cancer with any form of estrogen taken in any form. That isn't necessarily true, especially if estrogen is begun close to the start of menopause in your estrogen window.[59] According to the American College of Obstetricians and Gynecologists (ACOG), there is no evidence that local vaginal estrogen increases the risk of either death or recurrence of breast cancer in women with a history of breast cancer, even in estrogen-receptor positive breast cancer cases, though they do recommend trying non-estrogen options first.[60] Even if you're not a cancer survivor, some gynecologists will highlight the benefits of HRT, others discourage using it. That's why it is so important to work with a knowledgeable person who can help you individualize your treatment options.

Women are Unsure of Best Treatments

Knowing what to do can be challenging. Intuitively, one would think menopause is so common and there are so many treatments, it should be easy to get information, guidance, and treatment. However, that's not the case. It's not even close. Women quickly discover how hard it can be to get good and accurate information about menopause and its treatments from the medical community.

Here is the sad truth. Few doctors are adequately trained in menopause and doctor's visits are getting shorter and shorter. According to the New England Journal of Medicine, most primary care residency programs in the United States don't provide adequate education in women's health in general or in menopause management in particular,[61] and fewer than one in five Ob/Gyn residents receive formal training in menopause.[62] As a result, many patients find themselves searching the internet for information. And Dr. Google only has search engine training. As a result, many women are finding half-truths, partial truths, myths and misunderstandings that muddle their ability to take appropriate action. Women feel frustrated by all the contradictions they face from their healthcare providers, the misinformation circulating on the internet, and the wives tales they've heard from their friends and relatives. What results is often incorrect treatment, fear of treatment, no treatment or inaction.

Bottom line

An increasing number of women at work are either in or near menopause. Their symptoms are affecting their lives, their relationships and their work. But few workplaces offer either information or support for menopause in the workplace. As a result, far too many women are leaving their jobs or lessening their time at work. The good news is that change is possible and doable—there are excellent treatments and support methods that can make all the difference. And that will be good for women and for business. A list of certified menopause experts is available at NAMS.org. We also provide coaching at MenopauseCoaching.com.[63]

CHAPTER 6

A Menopause Policy Makes Sense…And Dollars

If businesses understood that menopause support saved them money, their only question would be, "Why aren't we doing this."

–Mache Seibel, MD

This is not rocket science. Employees who are rested, in shape, clear thinking, and calm feel healthier and perform better than those who are tired, out of shape, foggy, and anxious. Money spent on your employees' health isn't lost, it's invested. Companies do realize improving employee health is good for business. There are programs for pregnancy, lactation and childcare. But almost none have extended the support to include the next phases of a woman's life where nearly half of women at work live: perimenopause and menopause. Support is badly needed. According to an AARP survey of more than four hundred women ages fifty to fifty-nine about their menopause experience, menopause is alive but not doing so well. Eighty-four percent of women surveyed say their symptoms interfere with their lives, and twelve percent say they interfere a great deal or are debilitating.[64]

According to AARP, the most common symptoms of menopause for women:

- 50% hot flashes
- 42% night sweats
- 38% vaginal dryness
- 42% say they've never discussed menopause with a health provider
- Only 1 in 5 received a referral to a menopause specialist
- 60 percent of women with significant menopausal symptoms seek medical attention, but nearly three-quarters of them are left untreated[64]

It would be reason enough to address the menopause experience if it were just a significant cause of unpleasant symptoms that often affect work. But not addressing the menopause experience also carries health risks. Menopause has been clearly shown to accelerate biological aging,[65] increase brain vulnerability to brain aging and the risk of Alzheimer's Disease,[66] increase the risk of heart disease,[67] and the risk of osteoporosis or thinning of the bones, among others. By overlooking the needs of their perimenopause and menopause employees, businesses are not only missing the opportunity to help them feel better and perform better, but also to be healthier long-term. And that impacts the bottom line. It's a major reason companies support health related programs. It's a no brainer—perimenopause and menopause programs should be added to existing ones already provided.

Calculating the Cost of Not Addressing Menopause

According to Bloomberg Equality, the global impact of menopause on productivity is costing businesses over one hundred fifty billion a year.[68] That's based on a report from Reenita Das, a partner and senior vice president for healthcare and life sciences at the consulting firm Frost & Sullivan.

When you add in the additional costs to the healthcare system, Ms. Das estimates, the total price tag of menopause is over $810 billion globally. Those numbers will continue to rise because in 2030, a quarter of the world's female population will be menopausal. That's an astounding number considering the Bloomberg report only included women ages forty-five to fifty-five, which is often the ages when symptoms start. Using those ages, Ms. Das reports that women in menopause account for 11 percent of the workforce in the Group of Seven most-industrialized nations, and have steadily risen over the last three decades. We believe these numbers are in fact much larger. Up to ten percent of women enter menopause before age forty-five, and the symptoms can start up to a decade before that. In addition, some women won't enter menopause until after age fifty-five, and some of those will continue having symptoms for another decade.

These increasing numbers are finally getting some attention.[69] To quantify the economic impact of these numbers, studies have begun using a term called menopause's "economic burden for employers." To help calculate the economic burden of menopause on work, the UK borrowed terminology from labor economics. They use two terms.

1. **Extensive margin of the labor force** refers to women who leave, or lose their jobs earlier than they would have without bothersome symptoms. These costs include the costs of hiring and training a replacement employee, lost productivity due to the new worker's inexperience, or because the employer no longer has access to the former workers' institutional knowledge and history the worker takes with them.[70]

2. **Intensive margin of the labor force** refers to the group of women who choose to remain in employment and cope with their symptoms, which include reduced work hours, sick leave, lateness, and medical appointments. The report by Joanna Brewis, et al in 2017 discovered that women in this

group were more likely to be treated negatively by employers, managers and co-workers and less likely to be promoted.[69]

The Costs of Menopause Transition for Women's Economic Participation

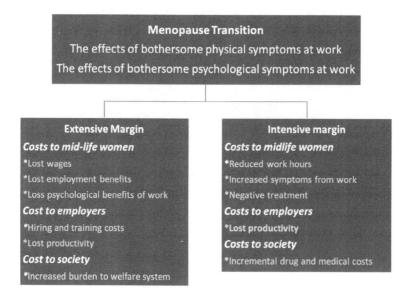

Modified from: Brewis J, et al. The effects of menopause transition on women's economic participation in the UK. Department for Education, London, 2017.[70]

Daysal and Orsini wrote a paper on extensive margin of the labor force for the UK Department of Health based on the US population.[71] In a sample of 21,732 respondents between the ages of forty and fifty-five, they documented that US women who discontinued the use of HRT following the WHI warnings about risks were thirty percent more likely to leave their jobs than those who continued with the treatment. That is a dramatic impact of treatment, or fear of treatment, on women dropping out of the workforce.

Two additional US studies evaluated the total costs associated with intensive margin costs of menopause on women in the workforce. Kleinman et al evaluated 17,322 working women having any type of menopause symptoms, and the same number without symptoms. Both groups were matched so that menopause symptoms were the main variable. Women with symptoms were found to have 40.7 percent higher annual health spending [higher medical ($4315 vs $2972, $p < 0.001$), higher pharmacy ($1366 vs $908, $p < 0.001$), take 21.3 percent more sick days with higher sick leave costs ($647 vs $599), and have 12.2 percent less hourly productivity and 10.9 percent lower annual productivity at work] than matched women who did not have menopause symptoms. The estimated annual incremental health spending per woman with symptoms was $2,042.[72]

A second study on *intensive margin* costs by Sarrel and colleagues in the journal Menopause examined the cost to businesses of women choosing not to treat their hot flashes. They reviewed the health claims of over five thousand women working in Fortune 500 companies who had one symptom—hot flashes. Half of the women were being treated for their hot flashes, the other half were not. During the twelve months of follow-up, the women with untreated hot flashes (252,273 women) were eighty-two percent more likely to go to the doctor for any reason, and 121 percent more likely to visit the doctor for hot flashes related issues. That ended up costing the companies $1,346 per woman per year in direct costs, and $770 in indirect costs ($2,116 per person per year in total). That translated into fifty-seven percent more lost days of productivity than the treated women.[73]

Hot flashes cost businesses nearly four hundred million dollars in this study of two hundred fifty thousand untreated women. Roughly thirty percent of perimenopausal, menopausal, and postmenopausal women have moderate to severe hot flashes.[74] If we were to amortize that cost over the number of women with moderate to severe hot flashes in the United States, the annual cost of untreated hot flashes alone would be roughly fourteen billion dollars, and that is just for hot flashes. Before reading this, if you were asked to guess what condition was costing the workplace fourteen billion dollars per year, there's a good chance the first thing that came to mind would not have been hot flashes. News flash!!! Hot flashes is the answer.

Even though hot flashes can have a huge negative impact on women's productivity, capacity to work, and work experience, some women will have a menopause experience that is greatly impacted by symptoms other than hot flashes. According to a review article of existing research reported in the British journal Maturitas, psychological and other somatic symptoms associated with menopause can have a relatively greater negative influence than hot flashes.[75] The menopause experience provides many symptoms capable of disrupting a woman's ability to work at her best or find a job.[76]

Other Costs of Not Supporting Menopause at Work

In the UK, studies have discovered that there are additional costs for businesses that do not support the menopause experience of their employees:

The cost of recruitment. According to Oxford Economics, replacing a woman who leaves the business costs over £25,000 ($34,750) for a person earning £30,000 ($41,700) a year.[77] That includes direct recruitment costs and bringing a new member of the team up to speed. In the United States, the cost for each person who leaves the business would have to include:

- Cost of hiring—interviewing, advertising, and temporary workers
- Cost of onboarding and training
- Cost of learning and development
- Cost of time with the unfilled role
- Cost of lost access to the former employee's knowledge[77]

Cost of absence. The UK Office of National Statistics has identified the highest rates of sickness absence included older women and those working in large organizations. It is highly likely that programs and policies supporting the menopause experience will lower sickness absence.[78]

Cost of employee relations issues or tribunals. In the UK, not supporting menopause has ruled in favor of the employee as a form of sex, age, or disability discrimination under the Equality Act 2010. The number of these cases is on the rise in the UK. It seems inevitable that these types of cases are highly likely to follow in the United States. The average cost of defending a tribunal case in the UK is £8,500 ($11,815), which if won, doesn't include the cost of any awards or the claimant's legal fees. It's also a big distraction from business, and a few of these could negatively affect the business's reputation.[79]

Menopause related complaints in the United States may fall under Sex or Age Discrimination (see Chapter 7). A 2017 National Bureau of Economic Research study found that older women are more likely to experience discrimination in the hiring process than their male peers.[76] The study suggested that the woman's aging looks may be to blame. According to the study, "Evidence suggests that physical appearance matters more for women, and age detracts more from physical appearance for women than for men." According to Helaine Olen of the Washington Post,[80] "Age discrimination begins to impact women years before menopause—one study pegged it at age forty for women."[81] All of this is really ageism, the Washington Post goes on to say, "it's not uncommon for middle-aged workers to attempt to hide their age in hopes of seeming younger to those in charge of hiring and firing."[80]

Ruth Finkelstein, executive director of the Brookdale Center for Healthy Aging at Hunter College, told the Wall Street Journal in 2019, "Older employees are in the closet today in much the same way gay employees used to be."[82] Helaine Olen concludes in her Washington Post article, "Few things say 'aging worker' like menopause, which the average woman experiences in her early fifties."[80]

Bottom Line: While not every woman will have a challenging menopause experience, many will. Failure to address menopause in the workplace is common and costly, accounting for billions of dollars in lost revenue for businesses, and future health issues for these women. Some of the cost is due to the impact of the menopause experience leading women to leave the workforce, some is due to the impact of the menopause experience on women's performance, some will be due to the impact of menopause on the future health of these women. All of this is amplified by the fact that menopause is a taboo topic with little or no support or education on the topic in the workplace. This contributes to losses for the business bottom line in the forms of having to rehire, absenteeism, and risk of employee relations issues or legal action. This latter point is in its infancy in the United States, but we predict that won't be the case for long. Businesses have the opportunity to take the lead, protect women and indirectly themselves, and become part of the solution.

CHAPTER 7

Menopause at Work and The Law

Common sense often makes good law.

– William O. Douglas

In 1978 Congress passed the Pregnancy Discrimination Act (P.L. 95-50-55), an amendment to the Sex Discrimination Section of the Civil Rights Act of 1964.[83] The law prevents harassment, provides light duty, maternity leave and other protections for pregnant workers. It also states that although pregnancy itself is not a disability, pregnant workers may have impairments related to their pregnancy that qualify as disabilities under the Americans With Disability Act (ADA). Amendments to the ADA made in 2008 make it much easier than it used to be to show that an impairment is a disability. Many of the women who went through pregnancy in 2008, or after were afforded some level of protection during their pregnancies. Those women in 2008 are now in their mid-forties, and it's not surprising those same women would expect to have at least some level of protection against discrimination based on their menopause experience.

However, in the United States, the area of menopause at work and the law is still in its infancy. There has been almost no focus on the legal requirements to support the menopause experience at work. But it is inevitable that it will happen. Here's why...

- About one fourth of the US workforce is in perimenopause or menopause
- Women in that age group are among the fastest growing demographic in the workplace
- Women are remaining in the workplace longer periods of time. The U.S. Bureau of Labor Statistics estimates there will be more than 55.1 million women fifty-five and older in the U.S. labor force by 2024.[84]
- An increasing number of women are transitioning into and through menopause during their employment years

From a practical point of view, women should be expecting and receiving more support from the workplace. According to one recent survey of 2,500 women in the United States experiencing menopause in the workplace:

- Ninety-nine percent of respondents are not provided with any menopause care benefits at work
- Symptoms with the most impact on work productivity include sleep disturbances (eighty percent), mood changes (seventy-eight percent), anxiety (seventy-five percent), brain fog/cognitive issues (seventy-five percent), and joint pain (fifty-two percent)
- Forty-five percent of women surveyed have had to take sick days due to menopause symptoms
- Sixty-six percent of respondents want access to a menopause specialist at no charge to the employees[85]

Who could perform at their best feeling tired, anxious, moody, foggy, and achy? Who would feel that their employer cared about them given the almost total lack of menopause support, awareness, or acknowledgement of their symptoms? Given this reality, it's easy to understand the negative impact the menopause experience could create for employers if they remain unaddressed. Women will inevitably feel employers are unsympathetic, unsupportive, and uncaring. Women will inevitably demand more, and some will seek legal remedies.

Jody L. Newman, an experienced employment lawyer with expertise in workplace bias against women, shared with us in an interview for this book that, "The UK is light years ahead of the United States in legally addressing menopause in the workplace and recognizes severe and long-term symptoms as a disability. In fact, there are so few cases in the United States related to this topic that it is essentially MIA."

The UK uses Employment Tribunals (ETs), independent judicial bodies who resolve disputes between employers and employees over employment rights. ETs may find direct sex discrimination if menopause symptoms are treated differently from other medical conditions, or if a man suffering similar symptoms would not have been ignored in the same way.

In contrast, US discrimination laws are based on broad protected categories such as gender, race, age, disability, sexual orientation, nationality, ethnicity, and others. "Issues with women in the workplace and menopause cut across three categories of US recognized discrimination – gender, age, and disability," according to Attorney Newman. "And so, where there seems to be some traction, not necessarily specifically menopause-related, but an avenue that's very amenable to this type of claim, would be something called 'intersectional discrimination,' where one or more types of protected categories collide to create a unique disadvantaged outcome."

Sex discrimination

Menopause could become an area ripe for sex discrimination in the United States if women are deemed treated less favorably than men with a similar condition. Alisha Coleman v Bobby Dodd Institute is an example of successful litigation based on sex discrimination and Title VII. Ms. Coleman was employed as a 911 call taker for the Bobby Dodd Institute, a job training and employment agency in Fort Benning, Georgia where she had worked for nearly a decade.[86] She was perimenopausal at that time and her menstrual bleeding was both irregular and heavy. The first event was heavy flow that resulted in Ms. Coleman soiling her chair. She reported the event to her supervisor, the Site Manager, who told her to leave the premises to change clothing, which she did. Approximately one or two days later, the Site Manager and the Human Resource Director gave her a disciplinary write up, and warned her "that she would be fired if she ever soiled another chair from sudden onset menstrual flow."

Ms. Coleman attempted to take extra precautions to ensure that another incident did not occur. However, a few months later, Ms. Coleman got up to walk to the bathroom and some menstrual fluid unexpectedly leaked onto the carpet. She immediately cleaned the spot with bleach and disinfectant. Soon thereafter, the Site Manager directed the Site Supervisor to relieve Ms. Coleman from duty, and the next day she was terminated. The stated reason for her termination was her alleged failure to "practice high standards of personal hygiene and maintain a clean, neat appearance while on duty."

Ms. Coleman filed a lawsuit that was initially dismissed. However, the ACLU of Georgia and co-counsel Buckley Beal LLP filed a brief in the Eleventh Circuit Court of Appeals arguing that their client, Alisha Coleman, was subjected to unlawful workplace discrimination when she was fired for experiencing two heavy periods while transitioning through perimenopause. The case was settled in 2018 for an undisclosed amount.

Sex plus Age discrimination

In 2020, the landmark case of Borstock v Clayton County,[87] Georgia was heard by the Supreme Court. In this case, Clayton County, Georgia, fired Gerald Bostock for conduct "unbecoming" a county employee shortly after he began participating in a gay recreational softball league. Altitude Express fired Donald Zarda days after he mentioned being gay. And R.

G. & G. R. Harris Funeral Homes fired Aimee Stephens, who presented as a male when she was hired, after she informed her employer that she planned to "live and work full-time as a woman."

Each employee sued, alleging sex discrimination under Title VII of the Civil Rights Act of 1964. The Eleventh Circuit held that Title VII does not prohibit employers from firing employees for being gay and so Mr. Bostock's suit could be dismissed as a matter of law. The Second and Sixth Circuits, however, allowed the claims of Mr. Zarda and Ms. Stephens, respectively, to proceed. The case was elevated to the Supreme Court which held that, "An employer violates Title VII for terminations based in part on sex. Pp. 9–12." The Bostock case led to a federal appeals court holding in 2020 that "sex plus age discrimination" is a legitimate basis for Title VII liability in court. Jody L. Newman, an attorney at the Boston Law Collaborative, shared with us in an interview that lower federal courts have long recognized particular subgroups of gender bias. "Women with young children was recognized as a unique form of gender bias in 1971. In 1979, another federal district court recognized race plus sex in a case involving a Black female plaintiff, where the court recognized that Black females are a unique subgroup protected by Title VII."

Attorney Newman continued that, "Sex plus Age had been deemed trickier because age discrimination is covered by a second federal law that's not Title VII, the ADEA (Age Discrimination in Employment Act).[88] Thus, there was some teeth-gnashing and hand-wringing about, 'Well, there's slightly different burdens of proof with age discrimination and Title VII.'"

"But the Bostock 2020 decision paved the way for Frappied et al v Affinity Blackhawk Gaming and set a precedent in the United States,"[89] according to Attorney Newman. "The Circuit court found that older women are subject to a unique kind of discrimination based on a combination of age and sex, which is distinct from either one alone."

In this case, several women at a casino alleged they were being fired and replaced by younger women due to age. The women successfully sued and demonstrated that workers can press so-called sex-plus-age theories alleging employers violated Title VII of the Civil Rights Act by discriminating against one subgroup of women including older women. "Under a sex-plus-age theory, just like Black women are a unique group, young are a group, women with young children are a unique group, so are older women. These 2020 legal developments would give a woman with menopause symptoms who is being treated differently, being discriminated against, being treated less favorably because she requires some assistance to work, or needs more breaks, or just the usual stuff that traditional employers consider to be a pain, would not be permitted," attorney Newman explained.

Demeaning and pejorative comments such as referring to a woman as an "old hag," "dried up," "forgot to take her hormones," etc. and menopause jokes, which are commonplace in many work settings, could also be deemed sexual discrimination. There have been successful harassment cases in the United Kingdom's ETs related to comments about recommending hormone therapy, or suggestions that a woman is "in a menopausal state." Comments like those should not and will not be tolerated in the United States either.

Employees [dealing with menopause] don't get the support they need. It is very difficult for women at work … it's ageism, it's sexism all rolled into one.

Conservative MP Rachel Maclean, August 2019 article in <u>The Guardian</u>.[90]

Disability discrimination

The issue of whether or not menopause is a disability is a very interesting one. In the UK, menopause is considered a disability under the Equality Act provided the symptoms have a long-term and substantial adverse effect on normal day-to day-activities. In a case tried in a Federal court in California, a woman experiencing menopausal symptoms sued in 2013 to be able to wear clothes that violated her workplace dress code, such as short sleeves and short pants, in order to feel cooler while at work.[91] The male judge ruled against her, stating that menopause was a natural condition and should not be viewed as a disability. We believe that as more female judges are appointed, it is likely they will bring a more open mind to these types of cases. As Attorney Newman put it, "Menopause might be an inevitable part of the human condition, but it's not inevitable that women have to suffer at work without reasonable accommodations." Under the Americans with Disabilities Act (ADA), this could change, particularly in certain instances of severe and long-term symptoms.[92] For instance, although menopause due to aging is a natural event, it could be viewed very differently if a woman were thrust into early menopause surgically, medically, or due to an illness, much like the Pregnancy Discrimination Act.

Under those conditions, induced menopause with the loss of child-bearing and the sudden onset of a severe menopause experience and its side effects could be viewed as a disability. Under the ADA, impairment is defined as any physiological disorder or condition, cosmetic disfigure-ment, or anatomical loss affecting one or more body systems, including the reproductive system. With those criteria, we believe that induced meno-pause will qualify as an impairment under the ADA. Induced menopause will likely create the test cases that influence whether menopause per se could be viewed as a disability under the ADA. The legal definition of a disability requires an impairment that has a substantial and long-term (at least twelve months) adverse effect on someone's ability to carry out nor-mal day to day activities. With symptoms typically lasting between three and ten years, menopause certainly meets the duration criteria.

That's why menopause programs and education and support are so important for the workplace. We'll talk more about this in Chapter 8. If employers view menopause as a medical condition, they can make reason-able adjustments for the workers and in the workplace environment, offer education, guidance, and support, and minimize the risk of being accused of discrimination based on a disability.

Women in the UK wanting more support for their menopause experiences are increasingly asking employment tribunals to settle workplace disputes for what they feel is a lack of attention to their needs.[93] They feel workplaces lack both the necessary practical support and the empathy required to support them as they transition into and through menopause.[94] Below are two employment tribunal cases outlined in the British publication Henpicked.[95] We have already seen the number of employment tribunal cases quadruple in the UK since 2018.[96] As you will see in reading these cases, it is highly likely that in the foreseeable future, these types of issues will lead to litigation in the United States, especially since case history, however scant, is in place. For that reason, addressing these issues is not only the right thing to do for women, it's the proactive thing to do for companies.

Merchant vs British Telecommunications (BT) (2012)

This was the first menopause tribunal case.[97] The employee, Ms. Merchant, brought a gender discrimination tribunal claim against her employer, BT, one of the world's leading communications services companies. BT alleged that her work performance was negatively affected by her severe menopause symptoms, which included significant stress and poor concentration. Her doctor wrote a letter that verified her claims.

According to one report, "the workplace management process required managers to examine whether underperformance was due to health reasons. In this case, Ms. Merchant's line manager did not consider the impact of menopause or request additional expert opinions. He chose instead to rely on his own experience and beliefs about menopause rather than to accept Ms. Merchant's doctor's beliefs."[95]

"She was fired and took the company to tribunal. The tribunal upheld her claim on the basis that the manager would not have approached a non-female-related condition in the same way. The tribunal also found the employer would have treated a man suffering from similar symptoms differently."[95] The tribunal wrote, "It is self-evident that all women will experience their menopause in different ways and with differing symptoms and degrees of symptoms."[95] Had the woman's manager been more informed about menopause, or at least more sympathetic, the outcome might have been different.

Davies vs Scottish Courts and Tribunal Service SCTS (2018)

This was the first menopause-related tribunal won on the grounds of disability discrimination.[98] An employee who worked as a court officer for the Scottish Courts and Tribunal Service (SCTS) was dealing with multiple menopause-related symptoms.[99] She was also being treated for a bladder infection with a medication she kept in her desk that required being dissolved in water. "Returning to her desk after a court visit, she found her personal items had been moved, the water pitcher on her table was empty, and two nearby men were drinking water. Because she was concerned, she warned the two men that the water could potentially contain medication."[95] Although the medication was not in the water, "the health and safety team subjected her to a rigorous investigation, which the tribunal felt went far beyond the issues it should have been examining. She was disciplined and dismissed from her job on the grounds of gross misconduct, which she unsuccessfully appealed. The tribunal ruled that the claimant was unfairly dismissed based on disability discrimination, and ordered that she be reinstated to her position, paid £14,000 ($19,460) to compensate her for lost pay between the dismissal and reinstatement, plus £5,000 ($6,950) in respect of injury to feelings."[95] We discuss the cost of ETs in more detail in Chapter 6.

Possible Laws in the Future

Imagine if the United States Equal Employment Opportunity Commission (EEOC) policies related to pregnancy, which apply to employers with fifteen or more employees, were amended to include what could be done for menopause in the workplace. Doing so would bridge the gap between a woman's reproductive life (infertility, pregnancy, maternity, etc.) and the rest of a woman's life beyond reproduction (perimenopause and menopause). It is amazing how well the EEOC policies below would apply if we just substitute the word "menopause" for "pregnancy." Below are major excerpts from the EEOC policies for pregnancy verbatim, with the exception of changing the word Pregnancy to Menopause and removing the word childbirth and references to nursing mothers. We believe it is only a matter of time before this occurs. The actual EEOC guidelines related to pregnancy can be found at https://www.eeoc.gov/pregnancy-discrimination.[100]

EEOC Policies Modified for Menopause

Menopause Discrimination

Menopause discrimination involves treating a woman (an applicant or employee) unfavorably because of menopause, or a medical condition related to menopause.

Menopause Discrimination & Work Situations

The Menopause Discrimination Act (MDA) forbids discrimination based on menopause when it comes to any aspect of employment, including hiring, firing, pay, job assignments, promotions, layoff, training, fringe benefits, such as leave and health insurance, and any other term or condition of employment.

Menopause Discrimination & Temporary Disability

If a woman is temporarily unable to perform her job due to a medical condition related to menopause, the employer or other covered entity must treat her in the same way as it treats any other temporarily disabled employee. For example, the employer may have to provide light duty, alternative assignments, disability leave, or unpaid leave to menopause employees if it does so for other temporarily disabled employees.

Additionally, impairments resulting from menopause may be disabilities under the Americans with Disabilities Act (ADA). An employer may have to provide a reasonable accommodation (such as leave or modifications that enable an employee to perform her job) for a disability related to menopause, absent undue hardship (significant difficulty or expense). The ADA Amendments Act of 2008 makes it much easier to show that a medical condition is a covered disability. For more information about the ADA, see www.eeoc.gov/laws/types/disability.cfm.[101] For information about the ADA Amendments Act, see http://www.eeoc.gov/laws/types/disability_regulations.cfm.[102]

Menopause Discrimination & Harassment

It is unlawful to harass a woman because of menopause, or a medical condition related to menopause. Harassment is illegal when it is so frequent or severe that it creates a hostile or offensive work environment or when it results in an adverse employment decision (such as the victim being fired or demoted). The harasser can be the victim's supervisor, a supervisor in another area, a co-worker, or someone who is not an employee of the employer, such as a client or customer.

Perimenopause and Menopause Leave

Under the proposed MDA, an employer that allows temporarily disabled employees to take disability leave or leave without pay, must allow an employee who is temporarily disabled due to menopause to do the same.

An employer may not single out menopause-related conditions for special procedures to determine an employee's ability to work. However, if an employer requires its employees to submit a doctor's statement concerning their ability to work before granting leave or paying sick benefits, the employer may require employees affected by menopause-related conditions to submit such statements.

Menopause & Workplace Laws

Menopausal employees may have additional rights under the Family and Medical Leave Act (FMLA), which is enforced by the U.S. Department of Labor.

Bottom Line: While not every woman will be challenged at work by her menopause experience, most will be affected to at least some extent. As a result, her work could be affected. In the UK, tribunals are already largely ruling in favor of women who file complaints. It is true that menopause is a natural event, but so is pregnancy. Induced menopause that occurs early for medical reasons may qualify as a disability in the United States. We predict laws will be passed in the United States to address menopause just as they have for pregnancy. It would be prudent for companies to take steps to future-proof their businesses and reduce their risk of litigation by offering menopause support and training for both the women experiencing the symptoms and the other employees who will interface with those women. In addition to serving as a legal protection for the company, it will improve employee retention, serve as a draw to top female employees, and ultimately, improve the company's bottom line.

CHAPTER 8

Moving the Needle

Optimize physical health to maximize fiscal wealth.

– Mache Seibel MD

If you are a business, you probably ask two questions before almost every decision: "Does it save money?" and "Does it make money?" No matter what the business, improving the bottom line is typically one of its top goals. That's why businesses invest mightily in new products (many of which flop or never make it to market), spend millions on advertising, buy up their competition at huge expense, and make many other costly investments. One of those other costly investments is employees. According to Delloite, American companies spent over one billion dollars on employee engagement in 2017 and over one hundred billion dollars on training and development activities.[103] Employees have access to health benefit programs on pregnancy, new moms, smoking cessation, mental health, weight control, sleep and others. When our daughter had her first child and initially had questions about breastfeeding, the company where she worked provided a lactation consultant.

Not every woman will conceive, be a new mom, breast feed, smoke, or need help with a mental health issue, weight control, or sleep—all important issues. However, every woman, if she lives long enough, will experience menopause. We are talking about roughly one fourth of the workforce, half of all working women. That is why supporting menopause at work makes sense, and dollars. Yet, in the United States, a national Menopause at Work survey found that only one percent of employers offer support specifically for women in menopause.[104] Although the UK is far ahead of the United States, and things are continuing to rapidly advance there, under one in ten companies in the UK have a policy, a program, or even mention menopause as part of their HR policy.[105]

Menopause remains such a taboo topic that most people are not even comfortable saying the word menopause. Several years ago the BBC reported that Dr. Andrea Davis from the University of Leicester was encouraging male and female university staff to overcome the discomfort of saying the word menopause by doing just that, saying "menopause" three times a day to remove the taboo and normalize it.[106] Along these lines, she also suggested women confidently announce in meetings when they are having a hot flash. You may or may not be ready to publicly announce in meetings that you're having a hot flash, but to her point, for things to change, people in the workplace have to start talking about an issue that is affecting a very large portion of the workforce.

Menopause is happening at work, and it's getting the silent treatment. Although some women are comfortable talking about menopause with their female co-workers, most generally are not comfortable talking about it openly or with their managers, and much of the workforce isn't even aware it is happening. It is time for companies to break the silence and address menopause for what it is – a natural event in all women's lives that can affect their work, their relationships, and their health. Ignoring menopause in the workplace is ignoring an opportunity to take action.

Creating Happy, Passionate, and Engaged Workers

The ideal business scenario is to have employees who are happy, passionate, and engaged at work. According to an executive summary by John

Hagel and colleagues from Delloite, there are three things that are crucial to create passion among today's workforce:

- the tendency to seek out difficult challenges
- the tendency to connect with others to find better solutions, and
- the desire to make a significant impact—drive the risk-taking that is necessary for this type of learning [103]

It is this kind of passion, the Delloite executive summary explains, that is crucial for a flexible, fast learning, and creative workforce that can sustain performance.[103] What company wouldn't want this type of workforce? From what you've learned in this book, it is understandable that anyone having a challenging menopause experience would have a difficult time channeling that degree of passion into work. Multiple studies and surveys have documented this fact, including ones demonstrating that women in menopause are dropping out of the workforce, reducing their hours, or choosing work that is less taxing.[107] Menopause is resulting in a brain drain of some of the most talented and experienced people in the workforce. In the UK alone, it's estimated that they could be losing 14 million work days a year related to menopause.[108] Since roughly half of the women in the workforce are in perimenopause or menopause, this is having a profound impact that will not change unless companies begin to future-proof their businesses. Doing that will result in a transformative change in the workplace.

Steps Necessary to Achieve Transformation
in the Workplace

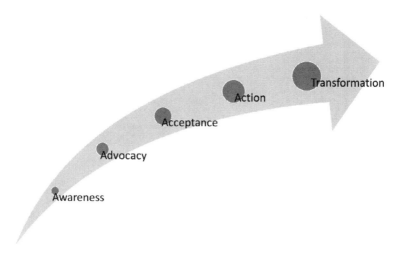

To significantly address menopause at work, shatter the silent ceiling, and achieve transformation requires a series of steps that begins with awareness. Awareness can come in the form of individuals experiencing symptoms at work, lectures, educational materials, studies, surveys, observations of employees, movies, television, online exposure, or anywhere people learn about a new concept. Awareness sets the stage for advocacy.

Advocacy happens when someone or a group realizes that something needs to be done about a situation. That can come in the form of self-advocacy (a person speaks up for oneself), individual advocacy (a person or group of people focus their efforts on just one or two individuals), and systems advocacy (changing policies, laws, or rules).[109] One UK menopause advocate, Pat Duckworth, author of Menopause: Mind the Gap, describes "Menopause Champions." These are voluntary personnel who do not need to be a member of HR or Occupational Health. The requirements for being a Menopause Champion are being clearly and easily contacted, enthusiastic about helping women at this stage, knowledgeable about menopause, and comfortable talking about it.[110] While such an individual would be an asset, a well-trained HR department should ideally have designated people with these qualifications. Similarly, some larger organizations may also provide a *Menopause Sponsor*—a senior management person who serves as a liaison between those implementing the menopause policies and the executives and organization committees.

When advocacy reaches a threshold, society begins to gain acceptance of a concept as needing to be addressed. Once acceptance occurs at the level of decision makers (either enough voters or people in charge), things spring into action that can lead to transformation. And like all overnight successes, it often takes years to pass through the stages of awareness, advocacy, acceptance, and action that leads to transformation. This doesn't have to be so. In the business world, CEOs can see something as a mandate, and use their position and influence to implement changes that lead to transformation in their company within a relatively short period of time. We'll offer examples of this in the next chapter.

Bottom Line: Businesses are worried about making more money, but almost none are aware that addressing menopause at work would help them achieve that goal. Addressing menopause symptoms would create a happier and more passionate workforce that would in turn impact the bottom line. There are a series of steps, beginning with awareness, that lead to the type of transformation that will future-proof companies.

CHAPTER 9

Lessons Learned from the UK

What you do makes a difference and you have to decide what kind of difference you want to make.

– Jane Goodall

The UK provides an interesting model to understand how menopause support in the workplace has been evolving. Although surveys of the impact of menopause symptoms at work were available nearly a decade ago, efforts to respond to those types of findings began to accelerate in 2016. That was when the Chief Medical Officer for England, Professor Dame Sally Davies, requested the Faculty of Occupational Medicine (FOM) to produce guidance on menopause and the workplace aimed at women going through menopause and experiencing the impact it has on their working lives.[111] Their report found that almost eight in ten menopausal women are working, and three out of four of those women experience symptoms. The report also revealed that menopause is the fastest growing demographic in the workplace. So it just made sense to provide workplace support for menopausal women. FOM also provided employers practical guidance on how to improve workplace environments for menopausal women, which were based on EMAS (European Menopause and Andropause Society) recommendations published in Maturitas.[112] The FOM President, Dr. Richard Heron, commented, "This is often a hidden health concern of working women, and it is so important that workers of all ages are better informed about how to confidently manage health issues such as this in their workplaces."[113]

A TV documentary was made from the FOM report to examine whether the UK workplaces were doing enough to support women, and the significant difference the right kind of support could make for menopausal women. The FOM report and subsequent documentary clearly demonstrated the need, and provided the awareness and impetus for change to take place.

As we described in Chapter 7, when enough people are clear about an issue and make enough noise about it, decision makers and politicians take notice. Spearheaded in the summer of 2019, MPs Carolyn Harris (Labour) and Rachel McLean (Conservative) called for women employees to understand what their employers could do to support them during the natural and universal transition of menopause. A lot of people are shocked to find that the transition into menopause can begin when a woman is in her thirties. It brings to light that many millions of women are on that journey and would benefit from knowledge, guidance, and support. The belief evolved that a menopause policy should be as common and available as a pregnancy policy.[114] Menopause advocacy has become a cross-party and cross-gender issue and a topic of discussion in the House of Commons. Men, especially those whose wives have been through it, understand and are supportive.

Dawn Butler MP, Labour's Shadow Women and Equalities Secretary, used a speech at Labour Party conference September 21, 2019 to announce that "the next Labour government would require all large employers to introduce a menopause workplace policy to break the stigma associated with the menopause as part of the party's plans to transform the workplace for women."[115]

Under Labour's plans, employers with over two hundred fifty employees would be required to:

- Provide training for line managers to be aware of how the menopause can affect working women and understand what adjustments may be necessary to support them
- Provide flexible working policies that cater for women experiencing the menopause
- Ensure absence procedures are flexible to accommodate menopause as a long-term fluctuating health condition
- Carry out risk assessments to consider the specific needs of menopausal women and ensure that their working environment will not make their symptoms worse.[115]

Employers could be required to make adjustments such as providing adequate ventilation, access to cold water, and giving women flexible working hours if their sleep pattern is disturbed.

The Labour MP Carolyn Harris told the Guardian:

You wouldn't dream of having a workplace where people weren't entitled to certain things because they were pregnant, and it's exactly the same for women with the menopause. I firmly believe there should be legislation to make sure every workplace has a menopause policy, just like they have a maternity policy. [116, 117]

Although the Labour party was unable to implement these measures, the UK is in the process of resurrecting this initiative by means of a petition to parliament and the government.[118] Anyone can sign the petition and it would require businesses with more than two hundred fifty employees to provide a menopause policy. Petitions that collect over ten thousand signatures require the government to provide a written response, causing the national government to make a statement. Petitions that collect over one hundred thousand signatures must be considered for debate, which would take the issue back to parliament. Parliament currently appears to have cross-party interest among both males and females.

Another initiative underway in the UK is being conducted by The Fawcett Society, which is a women's right charity.[119] They are surveying some three hundred thousand women in the financial sector from companies such as Barclays, EY, Legal & General and PwC to understand menopause as a workplace issue and how it can better be supported for that business sector. In addition to surveying women, "The Fawcett Society will include men, younger women and others who may either work with or manage them, as well as women of color and trans employees."[119] Again, awareness is leading to advocacy.

Taking a cue from Parliament and more generalized awareness, local governments in the UK are also taking action. Sadiq Khan, Mayor of London, as part of his recent re-election campaign, proposed a menopause policy at City Hall that would include a menopause leave for women affected with severe symptoms.[120] Mayor Khan now states he plans to implement this plan and expand it.[121]

As you can see, once sufficient awareness was raised, politicians and advocacy groups began to get on board. This is a necessary but slow process for change at the government policy level. On the other hand, businesses are able to take more immediate action. There have been a number of examples over the past several years. A number of businesses in the UK have begun introducing menopause policies into the workplace. One of the pioneers in this area was then forty-five-year-old Liv Garfield, the CEO of British water utility Severn Trent Plc., who in 2018 guided her company to become one of the pioneers of menopause education in the workplace. She was quoted in Bloomberg Equality as saying:

It's a way to demystify a natural phenomenon affecting menopausal women – – a growing cohort at companies around the world. With menopause driving scores of women out of the workforce each year, addressing it is essential.

To not employ swathes of women from forty-five to 60 has got to be a real issue – – otherwise you're missing all the insight from that particular generational category.[122]

Emma Walmsley, 52, chief executive of GlaxoSmithKline, had a very strong reason to understand that perspective clearly.[122] Half of Glaxo's female employees are over forty-five. In 2019 she also introduced a menopause policy at its global headquarters in the U.K. Around this time, with awareness of an important inequity in the workplace identified, and menopause support gaining momentum, the ACAS (Advisory, Conciliation and Arbitration Service: an organization in the UK that tries to prevent or solve problems between employers and workers) began to advocate for menopause support at work. On October 18, 2019, ACAS provided businesses some guidance for menopause support. Here are a few highlights from their suggestions:

- **Understand the symptoms of menopause**

  › feeling tired and lacking energy
  › hot flashes
  › anxiety and panic attacks
  › struggling to concentrate or focus
  › headaches including migraines

- **Tips for Best Practices to Manage Menopause At Work**

  › create and implement a menopause policy
  › provide awareness training for managers to deal with any concerns in a sensitive way
  › create an open and trusted culture within the team
  › make changes where possible such as altering working hours
  › implement low-cost environmental changes such as providing desk fans

› be aware of employment laws that can relate to menopause issues at work such as the risks of sex, disability or age discrimination[123]

The very next day, October 19, 2019, which coincided with World Menopause Day, the UK's Channel 4, led by female CEO Alex Mahon, issued a press release. They announced the launch of their new policy designed to support employees experiencing menopausal symptoms and guide colleagues and line managers about how to support those transitioning through it. It was the first media company to do so. Their goal was to end the stigma surrounding menopause by encouraging a better understanding of it among employees and facilitating a more open work environment:

> As part of Channel 4's menopause policy, women have access to flexible working hours, paid leave if feeling unwell due to menopause symptoms, including the sudden onset of symptoms while at work, a private, cool and quiet space, a working environment assessment to ensure that their physical workspace is not making their symptoms worse, and an array of support and guidance resources.
>
> The broadcaster is also introducing menopause awareness briefings to its leadership teams.
>
> Channel 4's HR team now has a dedicated Menopause Champion and the broadcaster's mental health employee network 4Mind, as well as in-house gender equality staff network 4Women, who are responsible for the new policy, offer a wealth of support.[124]

Other companies also stepped into the menopause support arena. Here are some large, recent additions that have made major commitments:

SANTANDER[125]

The Spanish bank Santander UK became an early provider of a menopause support initiative only days after the Labour Party Conference that announced their then radical plan to break the taboo of menopause in the workplace. Santander's roll-out plan began with a special awareness day on September 23, 2019 that transitioned into a program offering practical support and advice for the twenty-five percent of its female workforce in the menopausal age range.[126] The bank updated its communications with facts about menopause and shared sources of support with employees. In 2020, Santander added to its program the menopause support app Peppy as part of its benefits.

Santander UK's view on menopause is one that would benefit most businesses: menopause isn't just a women's issue, it is a workplace issue.

Sally Bridge, assistant secretary of The Communication Workers Union (CWU), the biggest union for the communications industry in the UK, said:

> I'm particularly impressed with the way that Santander has rec-
> ognized this isn't just a female issue. Men need to understand
> it better – and not just for the sake of their female line reports,
> because this is important knowledge for their domestic lives as
> well.[126]

As a result of their initiative:

- Seventy-five percent of participants felt their menopause symptoms were less bothersome
- Ninety percent of participants said they felt more positive about Santander as an employer
- This initiative led to Santander UK being named among the London Times top fifty employers for women in 2021

AVIVA

On October 15, 2020, the insurance company Aviva began running a menopause awareness campaign for UK employees. Activities included:

- Seminars aimed to support people experiencing menopause and those close to them
- Employees sharing their perspective with colleagues

Employees aged forty-five and over are the fastest growing employee population by age at Aviva. Numbers of women experiencing menopause in the workplace are growing overall.

To build on this, Aviva launched a smartphone menopause support app, by Peppy, freely available to all Aviva UK employees, which includes:

- A free forty-five-minute one-to-one phone consultation with a menopause specialist.
- Highly accessible, personalized live chat with a menopause expert through the app, providing reassurance at the touch of a button if people have questions or worries about symptoms or other issues.

A video created by Aviva shared quotes from employee interviews:

- I've worked at Aviva for some years. I've seen many changes but for me, going through the menopause has been a very difficult time.
- The menopause 'hit' me in my fifties, with symptoms that made me feel at times unable to cope with general day-to-day tasks.
- My phone consultation with a Peppy practitioner felt like I was talking to a friend. We talked about my symptoms and

medication and next time I spoke to my doctor, I felt empowered. I knew exactly what needed to be changed and why.

- I really appreciated having the opportunity to speak to someone else about my symptoms and how they were making me feel.[127]

In 2021, Aviva also launched menopause awareness training aimed at line managers, but available for everyone to help them support colleagues experiencing menopausal symptoms. Training covers:

- What is menopause
- Why it's important to talk about it
- Advice on how to support it

Leaders are encouraged to complete the training as part of this year's awareness campaign. Over one hundred fifty people had completed it at the time of their press release.

Aviva Norwich-based employee Emma Armes, who works in marketing and runs a menopause support group said:

People talk about hot flushes, but there's much more people don't talk about. One of the worst things is memory loss. When people learn that's a symptom, they're often relieved.[127]

Danny Harmer, Aviva's Chief People Officer, said:

We need to break the taboo of menopause. Most people are familiar with the common, and sadly sometimes still ridiculed, physical symptoms of menopause such as hot flushes and night sweats. Less well known are the mental health aspects, including anxiety and difficulty sleeping, which can have a massive impact on performance and self-confidence. So it's no wonder that one in four women consider leaving work because of menopause – a loss of talent that businesses can prevent[127]

Vodafone

Multinational telecommunications company Vodafone recently requested an independent study conducted by Opinium, surveying 5,012 people in five countries aged over eighteen who had experienced menopause while at work. Their findings revealed that:

- Nearly two-thirds of women (sixty-two percent) who experienced menopause symptoms said that it impacted them at work, rising to four in five (seventy-nine percent) for eighteen to forty-four-year olds.
- A third (thirty-three percent) of those who had symptoms said they hid this at work, and fifty percent felt there is a stigma around talking about the menopause.
- Forty-four percent of women who experienced menopause symptoms said they have felt too embarrassed to ask for support in the workplace, rising to sixty-six percent of women aged eighteen to forty-four.
- Two-thirds (sixty-six percent) of women agreed there should be more workplace support for women going through menopause.[128]

Vodafone estimates that menopause currently affects around fifteen percent of Vodafone's one hundred thousand employees. To ensure that all Vodafone employees feel comfortable seeking support, in March 2021 they initiated a global commitment that includes support and assistance, training, and awareness. The training and awareness program will be rolled out to all employees globally, including a toolkit focused on raising understanding of the menopause and providing guidance on how to support employees, colleagues, and family members. Existing policies in local markets will also provide support including the ability to take leave for sickness and medical treatment, flexible working and care through Vodafone's Employee Assistance.

Leanne Wood, Chief Human Resources Officer at Vodafone said:

"Vodafone's global commitment on menopause underscores our drive for a more inclusive culture and our desire for women to see Vodafone as the place to be for their career through all stages of their life. With menopause impacting women for a significant period of their working life, it's important to us that our environment supports and normalizes these life stages by openly talking about and supporting menopause in the workplace."[128]

DIAGEO

You may know this multinational beverage company more for its products like Guinness, Baileys, Smirnoff, and Captain Morgan. In March 2021 Diageo launched its first ever global Menopause Guidelines Thriving Through Menopause.[129] Initially launched across the United States, Canada, USVI, the United Kingdom, and Ireland, more countries are planned to follow.

The company hopes its guidelines will raise awareness and understanding of menopause, which is often a taboo subject. Diageo will provide resources to employees and line managers experiencing menopause at home or at work. In their press release, Louise Prashad, Global Talent Director, Diageo said:

We are committed to creating a fully inclusive and diverse workforce and as part of this to championing open and empowering conversations, particularly in subjects that can often be difficult or taboo. With today's launch of Diageo's Menopause guidelines we are actively encouraging all of our employees to build their understanding of how the menopause impacts women in the workplace and in our personal lives, as well as providing strengthened support and flexibility during what many women can find a challenging time in their professional careers.[129]

By 2025, there will be over one billion women experiencing the menopause in the world, equal to twelve percent of the entire world population. This highlights the importance and relevance of this topic as it is likely that everybody knows someone currently experiencing menopause.

Through the guidelines, tailored support will be available for women working across Diageo – from locations including its Guinness Open Gate Brewery in Baltimore, to those in the St James' Gate, Dublin, its global HQ in London through to many other locations across Canada, Ireland, USVI and the United Kingdom. Support mechanisms available include:

- Access to counselling or mindfulness sessions through the Employee Assistance Program (EAP)
- Increased flexibility where needed (e.g., changing working patterns, or access to sick pay entitlements to deal with symptoms where appropriate)

The guidelines have been created by a global working group, including members of Diageo's Spirited Women's Network resource groups, who have brought personal experiences, alongside best practice theory and external peer and partner company thinking together. Diageo has also recently been named No. 1 UK company for female leadership representation in the 2020 Hampton-Alexander Review[130] and recognized as a leading company globally for gender equality by the 2020 Bloomberg Gender Equality Index.[131]

Bottom Line: The UK has provided an interesting model for introducing menopause support into the workplace. It began in earnest when the Chief Medical Officer for England, Professor Dame Sally Davies, requested the Faculty of Occupational Medicine (FOM) to produce guidance on menopause and the workplace.[111] That led to women in parliament who understood the issues creating awareness in government that led to cross-party and cross gender support and advocacy in parliament. With that backdrop, local governments picked up the reins.

Subsequently, charities, the ACAS, and other organizations championed support of menopause work policies.[122] A handful of multinational businesses, recognizing the need, took action without government mandates by initiating menopause policies in their companies. Since many of these companies have branches in the US and other locations around the world, they will serve as a basis for entry of menopause support around the world.

We believe that this type of employee benefit will help to attract and retain women in perimenopause and menopause much the way companies with generous support of pregnancy attract and retain reproductive aged women today. It is reminiscent of when in vitro fertilization and other reproductive technologies first became available and women gravitated to companies that supported their needs. There is little doubt that companies wanting to future-proof themselves would be wise to adapt menopause policies to support one fourth or more of their workforce.

CHAPTER 10

Developing a Menopause Strategy

Good decisions come from experience, experience comes from bad decisions.

– Mark Twain

The United States is a global leader in medicine. However, she has a blind spot—accurate menopause information among the medical community and healthcare providers is disappointingly limited. In some ways it's not surprising. Medical training programs for primary care physicians and even for Ob-Gyn physicians in the United States allocate little time to menopause in general, let alone more specialized areas such as menopause in trans men and trans women, and menopause in women with chronic illnesses. While a minority keep up with the latest research and therapeutics in menopause because they are interested in it, the majority aren't sufficiently informed and often believe the same misinformation and myths as the lay public.

If that is the reality for US healthcare providers, imagine how little accessible and accurate information reaches the public at large, and the business community in particular. Sprinkle in the longstanding taboo surrounding menopause and reluctance to talk about it openly, and it's easy to understand why the menopause experience at work is being ignored in the United States. We predict that as the menopause segment of the workforce continues to increase, businesses will be forced to address this issue and develop menopause-friendly policies in order to attract and retain the best talent.

The tide is already beginning to change. Menopause is increasingly discussed in the media, menopause symptom relief products are now being advertised on TV and use the word "menopause," menopause femtech products are starting to populate the marketplace, and women politicians, celebrities, and CEOs are speaking up. Menopause is hot!

There are the six thousand US women who enter menopause daily and join their fifty million sisters already in it. Of note, the oldest millennials are turning forty this year. As a group, they are better educated, tech savvy, the largest group in the workforce, and the second-largest generation (after baby boomers) in the US electorate.[132] A formidable group is on the cusp of perimenopause. NAMS Medical Director Dr. Stephanie Faubion summed it up in an editorial.

> "This demographic of undertreated, symptomatic, menopausal women who find themselves in the menopause management vacuum have asked for, no demanded, that solutions be made available to them... They do not want to be treated like old women and believe that fifty is, indeed, the new thirty. These women are changing the conversation around menopause and are refusing to be defined by their fertility status."[133]

Companies should listen up and join the conversation. Women don't want to fall victim to their menopause experience. They want to remain vibrant and impactful in life and at work, and are looking to the workplace to see them for the value they bring to work every day—wisdom, experience, and perspective. They are weary from not knowing how best to manage their symptoms and are looking for answers. They don't want to be confused, immobilized, and uncertain what to do. They will increasingly be expecting businesses to respond to their needs with policies to support them.

What can businesses do?

Businesses need to become menopause-friendly. Two independent organizations in the UK are trailblazers in this area.

The first is the European Menopause and Andropause Society (EMAS). August 2020, EMAS issued a press release: Menopause in the workplace must become a global policy. They announced the establishment of World Menopause & Work Day. It launched September 7, 2021 with the intent of..."uniting to raise awareness on menopause in the workplace and fight for the reduction of the stigma and emotional burden attached to it. Menopause is a gender-and age-equality issue, and dealing with its consequences should be part of maintaining an inclusive environment."[134] The EMAS global consensus recommendations on menopause in the workplace and educational material can be found on their website.[135]

The second UK initiative is an independent menopause-friendly business accreditation movement spearheaded by Henpicked: Menopause in the Workplace. Henpicked offers accredited CPD (Continued Profession Development) courses and workshops on menopause, and certifies menopause-friendly workplaces that have met requirements established by their Independent Panel. Henpicked awarded their first menopause-friendly employer certificate of accreditation on June 25, 2021 to first direct, HSBC UK and M&S Bank.[136]

Separately, a menopause in the workplace inquiry was launched by a House of Commons committee to determine if the law should be changed to support menopause at work. That initiative has the potential of requiring businesses to implement a menopause policy. On this side of the pond, there is much to be done. Businesses can build on what we have learned from various elements in the UK—Parliament, the UK's research document entitled Menopause Transition: Effect on Women's Economic Participation,[137] UK based companies and organizations (see Chapter 9), the ACAS, and from the guidelines and recommendations put forth by the European Menopause and Andropause Society's (EMAS) journal Maturitas,[138] as well as studies published in the North American Menopause Society's (NAMS) journal, Menopause, and others.

Creating a Menopause Policy

A "Menopause Policy" sets expectations, policies, and procedures that are clearly spelled out. It allows everyone in a business to understand what menopause-friendly is, and what is required for that business to become menopause-friendly. At first this may seem like an overwhelming task. It can be. But it becomes less daunting when businesses view menopause as a normal part of the life cycle, and an extension of already existing health and safety policies. A menopause policy allows businesses to view menopause as a natural part of life that has not been acknowledged either adequately or appropriately in the workplace.

A menopause policy brings the menopause experience into focus as something that not only impacts a woman personally, but also has a potential impact on the business that employs her. It outlines supportive interventions that will positively impact a woman's menopause experience at work and her overall health. Unaddressed menopause symptoms can negatively affect a woman's future health, and an adverse work environment can exacerbate existing menopause symptoms, transforming the work environment into an occupational health problem. Lack of awareness of employment laws that can relate to menopause can lead to the risk of sex, disability, or age discrimination (see Chapter 7).[137] Menopause symptoms can create a productivity issue that can result in businesses losing revenue, and create an employee retention issue that can cost employers some of their most valuable and seasoned employees.

Before writing a menopause policy, it is helpful to confidentially survey the employees to discover specific areas of need. Most of what needs to be included falls into the following four headers:

1. **Company Culture** – The work environment needs to be safe, inclusive, and supportive for everyone.

   a. Highlight menopause awareness such as Menopause Awareness Month, World Menopause Day, and World Menopause & Work Day

   b. Provide ongoing information about menopause including options for reducing symptoms

   c. Appoint a Menopause Liaison to interface with employees, executives, and committees

   d. Require equality and diversity training[136]

   e. Allow flexible work hours, working remotely, absence and sick days. Covid-19 proved that online training, flexible hours, and working from home are an effective option in the workplace.

   f. Establish zero tolerance for jokes and negative comments about menopause

2. **Education and Training** – Who needs education and training about menopause? Everyone. From the CEO to HR. From the managers to the mailroom. Men and women. Young and old. Topics for discussion include:

   a. What is menopause

   b. Framing menopause as part of a woman's life cycle

   c. How menopause can affect women

   d. How menopause can affect performance

   e. How adjustments can make a difference

   f. Ongoing updates about new developments

g. How to have a supportive conversation with women about menopause and symptoms they may be experiencing

3. **Menopause Support Access** – Optimum support takes a village that involves Human Resources, peer-to-peer groups, coaching, and menopause healthcare providers.

    a. Provide Human Resource support that is knowledgeable about menopause, accessible, and able to both implement company policies and facilitate access to menopause support.

    b. Establish menopause peer-to-peer support groups

    c. Provide access to menopause coaching support. Menopause coaching has been shown to increase self-efficacy.[138] Menopause coaching can provide guidance, address questions, and explain best practices. Coaching can also explain lifestyle changes that can lead to improvement of symptoms and offer knowledge to help the person become a partner with her healthcare provider.[139]

    d. Facilitate access to medical providers trained and knowledgeable about evidence-based menopause care via an on-site occupational health provider or a referral system. Cancer survivors going through menopause face an additional burden as do those who are transgender and will require additional support.[140]

4. **Work Environment** – Studies have shown that the work environment can be detrimental for a woman's menopause experience, particularly if she is symptomatic.[141] In particular,

hot flashes are made worse if they are experienced in a hot or poorly ventilated work space or in informal meetings. When that occurs, menopause becomes an occupational health issue. Below are suggestions that can improve the menopause experience.

a. Provide women control of their workplace temperature

b. Provide women control of their workplace ventilation

c. Provide women access to cold water and bathrooms in all work situations

d. Provide adequate breaks from work

e. Create safe, quiet space for women to relax when symptomatic, and provide free feminine hygiene products in restrooms

f. Adopt a menopause-friendly dress code, particularly if uniforms are required

g. Implement low-cost environmental changes such as providing desk fans

h. Make reasonable adjustments when an employer is aware (or should reasonably be aware) that an employee is placed at a substantial disadvantage as a result of an employer's policies or practices or a physical feature of the workplace.

Bottom Line: Women are increasingly expecting, even demanding, that their menopause experience be both supported and protected at work, and they increasingly view this expectation as a responsibility of the workplace. Identifying the nature and the scale of the problem and the extent to which the menopause transition is a problem is an important first step.

A menopause policy should be a part of every company's policies. It should incorporate attention to the company's culture, education and training, system of access to menopause support, and revision of the work environment to accommodate the needs of menopause. Addressing all of these issues will help to establish that the company is menopause-friendly, and committed to the potentially one fourth of its workforce in perimenopause and menopause. Failure to address these issues may negatively affect recruitment, retention, performance, and job satisfaction. It may also cost the company revenue and the risk of future litigation.

Conclusion

When we began writing this book, we knew that working through menopause was an unrecognized issue in the workplace, particularly in the United States. Until we delved deeply into the topic, we didn't fully appreciate how unrecognized. There is an enormous opportunity for business to change the work culture in a way that supports both women and businesses to the betterment of both. We hope that this book will be a resource and an impetus for that change. That would be a win-win.

Contact us

Drs. Mache and Sharon Seibel are available to discuss the contents of this book with businesses or organizations and offer coaching for working women and their employers. Contact them at https://drmache.com/contact-us/.

ACKNOWLEDGEMENTS

We would like to acknowledge the hundreds of women who have shared their working through menopause stories with us, highlighting their many challenges, businesses' lack of awareness, and the immense need for change. We would also like to acknowledge the bravery of a growing number of celebrities, CEOs, and politicians who have advocated for and given voices to women working through menopause.

We would like to specifically acknowledge the dedication and contributions of the North American Menopause Society (NAMS), The European Menopause and Andropause Society (EMAS), the outstanding researchers and clinicians around the world who have advocated for menopause in the workplace, the advocacy of the UK government in promoting this topic, and Pat Duckworth's book Mind the Gap, which focuses on the British experience. Special thanks to attorney Jody Newman for her invaluable input on menopause and the law, and to Karen Giblin, Shelly Glazier, Robyn Spizman, Steve Lishansky, Terri Port, and Drs. Mary Jane Minkin, and Holly Thacker, for reading the manuscript and offering comments, and. Dr. JoAnn Pinkerton for her thoughtful and thorough foreword. In addition, we would like to acknowledge the efforts of the press for keeping an eye on this space.

We believe that working through menopause is at the same place that pregnancy in the workplace was in 1978 – in its infancy. The time has come for the post-reproduction phase of women's lives to be as protected in the workplace as their reproductive life.

ENDNOTES

1 HotYearsMag.com

2 http://www.menopause.org/docs/default-source/2014/nams-recomm-for-clinical-care

Introduction

3 http://bit.ly/TheEstrogenFix

Chapter 1: The Many Faces of Menopause – Three Case Studies

4 https://marcommnews.com/older-women-and-menopause-negative-ly-stereotyped-by-the-media-according-to-um-research/

Chapter 2: The Silent Ceiling

5 https://www.bbc.com/news/world-42026266

6 https://hbr.org/2020/02/its-time-to-start-talking-about-menopause-at-work

7 https://journals.lww.com/menopausejournal/Abstract/2015/03000/In-cremental_direct_and_indirect_costs_of_untreated.5.aspx

8 https://www.pewresearch.org/fact-tank/2017/03/07/in-many-countries-at-least-four-in-ten-in-the-labor-force-are-women/

9 https://www.dol.gov/agencies/wb/data/latest-annual-data/work-ing-women

10 https://sports.yahoo.com/menopause-work-uk-employment-wom-en-gender-issues-230130408.html

11 http://hrnews.co.uk/new-survey-reveals-90-of-uk-workplaces-fail-to-offer-menopause-support/

12 https://www.sciencedirect.com/science/article/abs/pii/S0378512218303396?dgcid=raven_sd_recommender_email

13 https://www.washingtonpost.com/lifestyle/wellness/michelle-obama-menopause-hot-flashes/2020/08/20/736cb23c-e195-11ea-8dd2-d07812bf00f7_story.html

14 https://open.spotify.com/show/71mvGXupfKcmO6jlmOJQT-P?si=u4VvnBlIT_-ZQJNo8AXSc

Chapter 3: Menopause 101

15 https://www.fenews.co.uk/fevoices/17921-it-s-time-to-talk-about-the-menopause-at-work

16 menopausemgmt.com/cultural-differences-in-symptoms-and-attitudes-toward-menopause/

17 https://bit.ly/TheEstrogenWindow

18 https://www.ncbi.nlm.nih.gov/pmc/articles/PMC3580996/

19 MenopauseQuiz.com

Chapter 4: Estrogen, Menopause and You

20 http://bit.ly/TheEstrogenFix

21 https://www.sciencedirect.com/science/article/abs/pii/S0378512218303396?dgcid=raven_sd_recommender_email

22 https://ftp.iza.org/dp7993.pdf

23 https://jamanetwork.com/journals/jama/fullarticle/195120

24 https://jamanetwork.com/journals/jama/fullarticle/2653735

25 https://journals.lww.com/menopausejournal/Abstract/2020/08000 The_Women_s_Health_Initiative_trials_of_menopausal.14.aspx

26 https://jamanetwork.com/journals/jama/fullarticle/198540

27 https://www.bmj.com/content/345/bmj.e6409

28 https://pubmed.ncbi.nlm.nih.gov/32721007/

29 https://www.ncbi.nlm.nih.gov/pmc/articles/PMC4520366/

30 https://pubmed.ncbi.nlm.nih.gov/27716751/

31 https://www.forbes.com/sites/stevensalzberg/2021/04/26/should-more-women-be-taking-estrogen-recent-data-says-yes/?sh=1b-da351927d1

32 https://www.authorea.com/doi/full/10.22541/au.161873076.60547427

33 https://bit.ly/TheEstrogenWindow

34 https://www.ncbi.nlm.nih.gov/pmc/articles/PMC7454316/

Chapter 5: The Impact of Menopause on Women at Work

35 https://www.gov.uk/government/publications/menopause-transition-effects-on-womens-economic-participation

36 https://www.bls.gov/opub/mlr/2015/article/pdf/labor-force-projections-to-2024.pdf

37 https://www.hrmagazine.co.uk/content/comment/is-2021-finally-the-year-women-can-discuss-menopause-in-the-workplace

38 https://www.fenews.co.uk/press-releases/27700-majority-of-working-women-experiencing-the-menopause-say-it-has-a-negative-impact-on-them-at-work

39 https://journals.lww.com/menopausejournal/Abstract/2021/02000/Relationship_between_number_of_menopausal_symptoms.11.aspx

40 The impact of the severity of vasomotor symptoms on health status, resource use, and productivity J. Whiteley, et al. Menopause, 20 (5) (2013), pp. 518-524

41 <u>The impact of menopausal symptoms on work ability</u> M. Geukes, et al. Menopause, 19 (3) (2012), pp. 278-282

42 <u>Menopause-specific questionnaire assessment in US population-based study shows negative impact on health-related quality of life</u> R.E. Williams, et al. Maturitas, 62 (2) (2009), pp. 153-159

43 <u>https://www.maturitas.org/article/S0378-5122(20)30386-8/fulltext</u>

44 <u>https://www.maturitas.org/article/S0378-5122(21)00107-9/fulltext</u>

45 http://www.tuc.org.uk/workplace/tuc-6316-f0.pdf

46 Stachenfeld NS. Hormonal changes during menopause and the impact on fluid regulation. Reprod. Sci., 21 (5) (2014), pp. 555-561

47 <u>Distress and coping with hot flushes at work: implications for counsellors in occupational settings</u> F. Reynolds Counselling Psychology Quarterly, 12 (4) (1999), pp. 353-361

48 Williams RE, Kalilani L, DiBenedetti DB, Zhou X, Fehnel SE, Clark RV. Healthcare seeking and treatment for menopausal symptoms in the United States. Maturitas 2007;58:348-358

49 <u>Griffiths A, et al: Menopause at work: An electronic survey of employees' attitudes in the UK. Maturitas 76 (2013) 155-159</u>

50 <u>https://www.sciencedirect.com/science/article/pii/S2214911221000242?dgcid=raven_sd_recommender_email#bb0035</u>

51 <u>https://doi.org/10.1016/j.crwh.2021.e00306</u>

52 https://www.washingtonpost.com/opinions/2021/06/28/is-menopause-really-driving-women-out-workforce/

53 <u>https://www.pfizer.com/news/press-release/press-release-detail/new_survey_highlights_the_impact_of_menopausal_symptoms_on_women_in_the_workplace</u>

54 <u>https://www.eurekalert.org/pub_releases/2020-12/tnam-nsl120120.php</u>

55 https://www.acas.org.uk/menopause-at-work

56 Griffiths A, Cox S et al. Women police officers: Ageing, work and health. Bordon: British Association of Women in Policing, 2006. ohaw.co/1ccYg9s

57 https://www.theguardian.com/membership/2019/sep/21/breaking-the-menopause-taboo-there-are-vital-stories-we-should-continue-to-pursue

58 https://www.acas.org.uk/archive/menopause-at-work#Impact%20of%20the%20menopause%20on%20a%20worker

59 https://www.amazon.com/Estrogen-Window-Breakthrough-Balanced-Through-Perimenopause/dp/1623366747

60 https://www.acog.org/news/news-releases/2016/02/acog-supports-the-use-of-estrogen-for-breast-cancer-survivors

61 http://allmediadownloads.s3.amazonaws.com/NEJM+Manson+paper+p1514242.pdf

62 https://pubmed.ncbi.nlm.nih.gov/23632655/

63 MenopauseCoaching.com

Chapter 6: A Menopause Policy Makes Sense…And Dollars

64 https://www.aarp.org/health/conditions-treatments/info-2018/menopause-symptoms-doctors-relief-treatment.html

65 https://www.ncbi.nlm.nih.gov/pmc/articles/PMC4995944/

66 https://journals.plos.org/plosone/article?id=10.1371/journal.pone.0207885

67 https://www.ahajournals.org/doi/full/10.1161/CIR.0000000000000912

68 https://www.bloomberg.com/news/articles/2021-06-18/women-are-leaving-the-workforce-for-a-little-talked-about-reason

69 https://www.gov.uk/government/publications/menopause-transi-

tion-effects-on-womens-economic-participation

70 https://www.higheredjobs.com/articles/articleDisplay.cfm?id=468

71 Daysal NM and Orsini C (2014) 'The miracle drug: hormone replacement therapy and the labor market behavior of middle-aged women' IZA Discussion Paper Series: number 7993

72 https://pubmed.ncbi.nlm.nih.gov/23532198/

73 https://journals.lww.com/menopausejournal/Abstract/2015/03000/ Incremental_direct_and_indirect_costs_of_untreated.5.aspx

74   https://jamanetwork.com/journals/jamainternalmedicine/fullarticle/410513

75   https://www.maturitas.org/article/S0378-5122(15)30090-6/abstract%20

76 https://www.nber.org/system/files/working_papers/w21669/w21669.pdf

77 https://bit.ly/OxfordEconomicsBrainDrainCost

78 https://www.ons.gov.uk/employmentandlabourmarket/peopleinwork/labourproductivity/articles/sicknessabsenceinthelabourmarket/2018

79 https://www.accountsandlegal.co.uk/small-business-advice/employment-tribunals-costing-uk-employers-8-500-on-average

80 https://www.washingtonpost.com/opinions/2021/06/28/is-menopause-really-driving-women-out-workforce/

81 https://www.ft.com/content/e4141576-04eb-11e9-99df-6183d3002ee1

82 https://www.wsj.com/articles/older-workers-have-a-big-secret-their-age-11574046301

Chapter 7: Menopause at Work and The Law

83 https://www.eeoc.gov/laws/guidance/fact-sheet-small-businesses-pregnancy-discrimination

84 https://www.bls.gov/opub/mlr/2015/article/labor-force-projections-to-2024.htm

85 https://www.businesswire.com/news/home/20210708005184/en/New-Survey-from-Gennev-Reveals-the-Impact-Menopause-Has-on-Productivity-in-the-Workplace

86 https://law.justia.com/cases/federal/appellate-courts/ca10/19-1063/19-1063-2020-07-21.html

87 https://www.scotusblog.com/case-files/cases/bostock-v-clayton-county-georgia/

88 https://www.eeoc.gov/statutes/age-discrimination-employment-act-1967

89 https://law.justia.com/cases/federal/appellate-courts/ca10/19-1063/19-1063-2020-07-21.html

90 https://www.theguardian.com/society/2019/aug/25/mandatory-workplace-menopause-policies-uk

91 https://www.laboremploymentreport.com/2013/10/18/menopause-is-not-a-disability/

92 https://askjan.org/publications/consultants-corner/vol09iss01.cfm

93 https://www.theguardian.com/uk-news/2021/aug/07/menopause-centre-increasing-number-uk-employment-tribunals

94 https://journals.sagepub.com/doi/abs/10.1177/0950017011426313

95 https://menopauseintheworkplace.co.uk/employment-law/tribunals-employers-best-practice/

96 https://www.covermagazine.co.uk/news/4035721/employment-tribunals-increasingly-concerning-menopause

97 https://www.thehrdirector.com/legal-updates/legal-updates-2012/failure-to-address-menopause-amounted-to-sex-discrimination/

98 https://www.peoplemanagement.co.uk/news/articles/tribunal-win-dis-missed-medication-muddle#gref

99 https://assets.publishing.service.gov.uk/media/5afc31a8ed915d0d-e80ffd2c/Ms_M_Davies_v_Scottish_Courts_and_Tribunals_Ser-vice_4104575_2017_Final.pdf

100 https://www.eeoc.gov/pregnancy-discrimination

101 http://www.eeoc.gov/laws/types/disability.cfm

102 http://www.eeoc.gov/laws/types/disability_regulations.cfm

Chapter 8: Moving the Needle

103   https://www2.deloitte.com/us/en/insights/topics/talent/fu-ture-workforce-engagement-in-the-workplace.html/#endnote-1

104 https://www.corporatewellnessmagazine.com/article/mak-ing-space-workplace-menopause-education#:~:text=By%202020%2C%20it's%20estimated%20that,which%20can%20affect%20work%20perfor-mance.

105 http://hrnews.co.uk/new-survey-reveals-90-of-uk-workplaces-fail-to-offer-menopause-support/

106 https://www.bbc.com/news/uk-england-leicestershire-45269434

107 https://www.bloomberg.com/news/articles/2021-06-18/women-are-leaving-the-workforce-for-a-little-talked-about-reason

108 https://www.hrreview.co.uk/hr-news/menopause-costs-uk-economy-14-million-working-days-per-year/115754

109 http://cedwvu.org/resources/types-of-advocacy/

110 Duckworth P. Menopause: Mind The Gap. The Value of Supporting Women's Wellness in the Workplace. HWCS Publications. England. 2020.

Chapter 9: Lessons Learned From the UK

111 https://www.fom.ac.uk/health-at-work-2/information-for-employers/

dealing-with-health-problems-in-the-workplace/advice-on-the-menopause

112 https://core.ac.uk/reader/33575847?utm_source=linkout

113 https://medicalxpress.com/news/2016-11-guidance-menopause-workplace.html

114 https://www.theguardian.com/society/2019/aug/25/mandatory-workplace-menopause-policies-uk

115 https://labour.org.uk/press/labour-announces-plans-break-stigma-menopause-work/

116 https://www.theguardian.com/society/2019/aug/25/mandatory-workplace-menopause-policies-uk

117 https://www.theguardian.com/money/maternitypaternityrights

118 https://www.positivepause.co.uk/all-blogs/menopause-workplace-policy-a-new-petition

119 https://www.theguardian.com/society/2021/may/19/financial-sector-takes-part-in-survey-about-impact-of-menopause

120 https://metro.co.uk/2021/04/27/sadiq-khan-backs-world-leading-menopause-plan-which-may-give-women-time-off-14474369/

121 https://www.independent.co.uk/news/uk/home-news/menopause-policy-sadiq-khan-mayor-b1838742.html

122 https://www.bloomberg.com/news/articles/2021-06-18/women-are-leaving-the-workforce-for-a-little-talked-about-reason

123 https://www.acas.org.uk/guidance-for-employers-to-help-manage-the-impact-of-menopause-at-work

124 https://www.channel4.com/press/news/channel-4-launches-dedicated-menopause-policy

125 https://employeebenefits.co.uk/santander-uk-supports-people-

through-menopause/

126 https://www.cwu.org/news/santander-leading

127 https://www.aviva.com/newsroom/news-releases/2020/10/aviva-launches-new-workplace-menopause-support/

128 https://www.vodafone.com/news/press-release/vodafone-announces-new-global-employee-commitment-menopause

129 https://www.diageo.com/en/news-and-media/press-releases/diageo-introduces-global-menopause-awareness-guidelines/

130 https://www.diageo.com/en/news-and-media/features/diageo-named-no-1-uk-company-for-female-leadership-representation-in-2020-hampton-alexander-review/

131 https://www.diageo.com/en/news-and-media/features/diageo-included-in-2020-bloomberg-gender-equality-index/

Chapter 10: Developing a Menopause Strategy

132 https://www.pewresearch.org/social-trends/2019/02/14/millennial-life-how-young-adulthood-today-compares-with-prior-generations-2/

133 https://journals.lww.com/menopausejournal/Fulltext/2021/04000/Femtech_and_midlife_women_s_health__good,_bad,_or.1.aspx

134 https://www.emas-online.org/emas-and-menopause-in-the-workplace-2021/world-menopause-and-work-day/

135 https://www.emas-online.org/emas-and-menopause-in-the-workplace-2021/

136 https://mailchi.mp/0e93f5106e45/your-exclusive-festive-invitation-2080922?e=5ca8720e68

137 https://www.gov.uk/government/publications/menopause-transition-effects-on-womens-economic-participation

138 https://www.maturitas.org/action/showPdf?pii=S0378-5122%2821%2900107-9

139 https://www.tandfonline.com/doi/abs/10.1080/08952841.2015.1137434

140 https://www.sciencedirect.com/science/article/pii/S0378512213002235

141 https://theconversation.com/menopause-discrimination-is-a-real-thing-this-is-how-employers-can-help-108641